THE SCIENCE OF PERSONAL COACHING

A formula for powerful life and business coaching conversations

BY CYNDI D. MCCOY

Psst... If you enjoy my work, check out more products and services at:

www.BestKindaFriend.com

A Best Kinda Friend ™ - there for you on demand or with a booking 24/7.

and

www.BoundariesCheck.com

The only boundaries book you'll ever need. Also an app, live challenges, and more.

Dedication

To the one who makes a way when there is no way.

CONVOSIQUE

The Science of Personal Coaching
Edition - Third
Publisher name: Convosique Pty. Ltd.
Website: http://www.convosique.com
Email: hi@convosqiue.com

Legal statements

To make the lawyers happy, I've made sure to include some important legal disclaimers below.

By reading this book, readers assume 100% responsibility and full ownership of their actions and the outcomes of their decisions or actions based on the material in this book, including any damages or adverse consequences that may arise from those decisions or actions.

The opinions and theories of the author of this book in general and the opinions and theories contained in this book specifically do not represent the opinions and theories of anyone or any organization quoted in this book or referenced, unless explicitly stated.

Every effort has been made to obtain permissions, properly credit, and acknowledge sources for the content of this book. If any permissions, credit, or acknowledgments have been overlooked or omitted, or any rights overlooked, it is unintentional. Please notify the publisher, and it will be rectified in future editions.

This book may be purchased for educational or business use.

The Science of Personal Coaching is an intended trademark of Convosique Pty. Ltd.

Some editing work in this edition provided by Beth Claire de Wet and Martha Mearns.

To ask anything about the above, please contact the publisher using the contact information provided.

CONTENTS

IS THIS BOOK FOR YOU?

AN INTRODUCTION

Hi there! I'm Cyndi, and in protest of the typical sterile-collared-shirt author photo, here is a selfie of me lying down on my pineapple-patterned meditation mat on my floor in Sydney, Australia, where I lived when I published this book's first edition.

Welcome to *The Science of Personal Coaching*. I wrote this book in order to pass on to you a step-by-step formula so that you can create the life-changing power of personal coaching - like a scientific process in which two elements combine to form a far more powerful and transformative solution.

You can use it in the lives of your family, friends, or work colleagues. You can also repeat this transformative process in the internal dialogue of your own mind to coach yourself. And, if you choose to make it a profession, you can use the same process in this book as the structure of every conversation with your professional coaching clients.

I am passing these coaching skills and techniques on to you because of the power it will give you to get "unstuck" in any area of life and help others get unstuck, too.

Coaching is magical. But even magicians have a secret process they follow behind-the-scenes, and so I'm here to take you behind the curtains.

Note that wherever I say "coaching," I mean "personal coaching," which covers both life and business coaching.

We're at an interesting time in history in which the coaching profession is fairly new, and so it's not yet highly regulated. That means there is a large spectrum of skills, price tags, and professional qualifications. On one end of that spectrum, there are top educated and credentialed life coaches who charge thousands of dollars an hour and work with celebrities, top-ranking CEOs, and other affluent clients; they tend to offer bespoke coaching services with very high price tags.

On the other end of the spectrum, there are unqualified and ineffective coaches who have slapped on themselves the title of "coach" with little or no genuine skills or techniques under their belt.

Those coaches who understand the powerful tools, skills, and techniques at a professional level have drastically improved the quality of life, decisions, and actions for so many of their clients.

For me personally, coaching has had a profoundly positive impact on most decisions I have made in all areas of my life, including career choices, dating, income, and health.

I am a coach, and I also hire a personal coach on a regular basis. I love every coaching conversation.

A coach helped me completely overcome a consistent feeling of anxiety I used to feel in my chest every time I looked at my bank account. A coach also then helped me receive two amazing and consecutive pay increases. The first jump was 37.5% more than I was making at the last job, and then my next job provided another 41% increase on top of that.

What else has coaching done for me? I was able to get my dream job title. I was able to overcome and successfully manage a body image disorder. I found hope and then a cure for a very serious illness. I turned an overwhelmingly stressful relationship into a peaceful one with healthy boundaries. I overcame my own belief in what someone I loved had said about a dream of mine, "You won't finish that." But with coaching, I finished it. I turned a very unhealthy cycle of dating decisions and what I "don't want" into a healthy and defining list of exactly what I "do want" - and most importantly what I need - from a partner, which turned into a dramatically positive life-changing decision.

The results go on and on... and on.

After working with quite a few coaches throughout the years, I have so many more stories of realizing I could do what I didn't think I could do.

I studied coaching and developed the theory in this book because of the incredible experiences I had as a coaching client.

Through the process of becoming a credentialed coach with the International Coach Federation, I was humbled by my clients' results. Their coaching needs cover vastly different areas of life, and some examples of their results include:

... fulfilling a dream to travel the world after a big financial obstacle,

... sparking fiery sexual intimacy in what was a dull and sexless relationship,

... improved happiness at work, despite a difficult manager,

... a partner saying "I love you" for the first time after desperately needing to hear it,

... a switch to a far more fulfilling career,

... a complete overhaul of diet and exercise in the life of someone who didn't think they could do it,

... and so many more.

Because of the dramatic changes I saw - both as a client of a coach and as a paid professional personal coach - I had an irresistible need to discover the process and science behind it.

While all the coaching programs I've seen or completed *did* give me great information and principles for coaching, the sad part was that none of those programs seemed to provide a chronological order of all the boxes to tick in each coaching conversation.

As a result of that major missing piece, many or most coaches I spoke with admitted to feeling lost in while talking with their clients, inwardly panicking, not knowing which way to go with the conversation. They had no formal process.

With my theory in this book, I fix that. In this book, I provide the chronological steps and process of each coaching conversation together with a checklist of what needs to happen in each of those steps.

If something in you lights up at the sound of anything that I've said so far, then this book is for you.

If you're still unsure whether or not this book is for you, then here are some questions and answers.

IS THIS BOOK ABOUT LIFE COACHING OR IS IT ABOUT BUSINESS COACHING?

You may have heard of the terms "life coaching" or "business coaching," but, "personal coaching" covers *both areas*.

This book is about *personal coaching*.

Personal coaching *encompasses the whole person* (linking business and the rest of life) because life and work have an unbreakable and necessary impact on each other.

A study published by Harvard Business Review Survey on Executive Coaching revealed that, although a company hires a coach for non-personal reasons 97% of the time, still 76% of coaches report that these clients bring up personal issues during their coaching conversations.[1]

76% is an overwhelming majority of coaches hired for executive coaching who then provide coaching around personal life. Why is that? Because effective coaching recognizes how interwoven career and personal aspects are in the tapestry of life.

It makes for an uncomfortably fake and irrelevant coaching conversation to pretend that life and business don't depend on each other. Integrity demands interdependency. The two have an unbreakable correlation, and all too often treating them as unrelated often causes anxiety that seeps out in the wrong places and situations, a sense of lying to oneself, a sense of a split personality, or much worse.

So, this book about personal coaching covers both. I believe the training in this book will prepare you to coach someone who needs business coaching as equally as someone who needs life coaching. The same rules, tools, and stages of a conversation apply to both topics.

Think of a "personal coach" as synonymous with a "life coach" and "business coach" or "career coach." All of them will follow the same conversation structure and process in this book.

Consistent personal coaching conversations change life, business, career, and everything in between. For example, many years ago, when I first heard of the term "life coach" I thought it was total BS, and when I made my first appointment to talk to one, I genuinely felt so embarrassed. I didn't want to tell anyone about it.

It was a friend of a friend's recommendation - not work related at all. But then, after the very first conversation, it changed my entire career and every other area followed afterward. My first conversation supercharged my belief in my capabilities and what I thought was possible for my life in all areas.

It was such a profound experience, so I set out to understand, step-by-step, what were the techniques and skills that my coach used to perform her magic. After years of study and analysis, I realized that there is indeed a *formula* - a specific *process of events* in a certain order - that makes the magic happen, and it's all now here in this book.

Both scientists and magicians - they both have formulas and processes to make wonderful things happen. It's the same with great coaching.

The front cover of this book shows a science experiment - two chemicals combining to create a beautiful reaction as two people have a conversation, because that's what a great coaching conversation does.

HOW WAS THE SCIENCE OF PERSONAL COACHING DEVELOPED?

Since 2008, I've been analyzing the process of a coaching conversation from the perspectives of both a coach and a client. I worked on identifying the key events that must happen - and in what order that they happen - for a client to see powerful change in each conversation. I worked through identifying the conditions that cause the sudden magical switch from utter disbelief in oneself to profound belief and action.

I found several coach-training programs were great at teaching high-level theory and coaching exercises, but they did not provide students a step by step formula or equation that I could follow to repeat the mind-blowing outcomes that I was experiencing. So, I observed and dissected the steps and patterns myself.

I figured it out, and now it's in the theory of this book.

Science is defined as a systematically organized body of knowledge on a particular subject, and that's what I have gathered after all these years. The training programs that I knew about had valuable knowledge, but it was not systematic or in any kind of practical and repeatable order that a scientific formula demands. So, I found what was lacking and systemized coaching.

Once I understood the process, I thought to deliver it as a metaphor that many or at least most readers could relate to. I took what I discovered as the seven "gears" of a personal coaching conversation, comparing it to the mechanical process of shifting the gears of a car to give it speed and performance at the right times.

There are many ways that the power, performance, and direction of a vehicle parallels the power, performance, and direction of a coaching conversation. And so, that's the central metaphor that I will introduce in this book - drawing a parallel to how a coach "drives" a coaching conversation, like a professional driver.

IS THIS BOOK ONLY FOR PEOPLE WHO WANT TO BE A PROFESSIONAL COACH?

This book is for anyone who wants to know what happens behind the scenes of a coaching conversation, regardless of whether you want to be a professional at it.

It's like knowing a few nursing skills vs. being a professional nurse. It's important to know how to bring down a fever or bandage a wound, and knowing those techniques doesn't make you a professional nurse, but knowing those things can help you save a life.

Likewise, learning even a few personal coaching skills in this book can help you powerfully affect someone's life, if or when the need arises. You can potentially "save" their emotional life with a single, powerful coaching question at the right time.

So, this book can also benefit you significantly, even if you don't want to practice coaching professionally.

The conversation techniques in this program show you how to ask provocative questions that no one else is asking - questions that trigger paradigm shifts, questions that make fear lose its suffocating grip on a person's decisions, and questions that move a person from a state of feeling stuck (knowing what "I don't want") to a state of motivation and clarity (knowing what "I do want").

HOW MUCH TIME DO I NEED TO INVEST IN THIS BOOK'S EXERCISES?

If you are lightly curious about coaching, then you might choose to skip completing the exercises in this book. Read chapters as you please, whenever you wish.

If you're more interested in a casual degree of learning, you can choose to skip some questions in a chapter's exercise and complete only those that intrigue you.

However, if you are passionate or excited about coaching or you love personal development or you wish to be a coaching pro, then complete all the exercises and record every one of the points that you earn.

Each question, or "Point" as they are called, in each exercise can range significantly in the amount of time and thought required. Questions in the first exercises might start off quick and super simple, but they soon become deep and meaningful, needing your dedicated time for reflection and practice.

If your plan is to learn coaching at a professional level, then complete the chapters and collect points with each and every exercise. These exercises will require dedicated chunks of time from you over the next several weeks or couple months, all depending on how you spread them out in your week. Some simple exercises may take just a couple minutes, while others might take hours because they require you to practice your skills with other people.

WHAT'S THE BEST WAY TO LEARN THE CONTENTS OF THIS BOOK?

The short answer is this: earn all the points you can in each chapter's exercise.

Now, here's the long answer.

As you walk through each chapter and complete its exercise, you'll need a dedicated notebook or journal (paper or digital) to write down (or type) your answers to questions and record a history of your points earned. It's your personal coaching diary, but I refer to it simply as "your diary."

It's inside of this diary where you record all your responses to exercises and challenges, and most importantly it's where you keep a history of your number of points earned along the way.

The points system you see throughout each chapter's exercise is there to keep you accountable and to create a fun and measurable way for you to track and quantify your effort and training. Some points will be quick and very simple to earn, while other points take a significant amount of reflection or time.

There is a total of **1,068 points** that you can earn throughout this book. The sum of 1,068 would be your total points only if you complete every question or challenge in every exercise in this book.

The great and perhaps surprising thing is that I designed exercises so that *there are no right or wrong answers*; rather, you earn each point only by doing the work, and by doing the work, you learn. Responding (in your diary) to each question and completing challenges give you valuable understanding of coaching.

Your number of points collected by the end of this book represents a record of your effort and practice of the coaching process and concepts. You earn points simply by completing your answers to questions and challenges the best you can.

Some chapters award a vastly different number of points; some short chapter exercises award 3 points, and the intensive chapter where you practice coaching over a longer period of time awards 880 points. By the end of this book, if you have earned all points, then as creator of this program, I consider you ready to start coaching professionally.

Several exercises will require you to return to your answers in an earlier chapter's exercise, and so it's important to *keep all your work in your one diary and keep it somewhere safe*.

For each exercise, start a new page or section titled with the chapter number and the day's date. Write the corresponding question number for each of your answers so that you can easily refer to it in later chapters.

In addition to keeping track of your points, keep in mind that chapters throughout *The Science of Personal Coaching* are cumulative, and so there is a very good chance you will not understand some of the terminology and ideas that you're reading if you skip a chapter or read it out of order.

So, the key is to start from the beginning, complete each exercise, and record your points earned.

Finally, from the next chapter (Chapter 1) through to Chapter 21, make sure to keep your diary with you each time you sit down to read. Exercise Chapter 1 will share everything else that you need to know about how to manage your diary.

CHAPTER 1, ANY QUESTIONS ABOUT COACHING?

Coaching is about you, the client. 100%. Because of that, I'll make you the focus of most of these chapters, and so several of the exercises in this book will aim for you to get clarity or take action in some area of your life.

By following this book and its exercises, you can learn what it's like to be a coach and a client at the same time. For the most part, I'll refer to you as the client.

But before we start focusing on you, an important first step in coaching is to get on the same page or agree on the terms of coaching and what you can expect to get out of it.

WHAT DO PERSONAL COACHING CONVERSATIONS LOOK LIKE?

Personal coaching sessions are simply a series of one-on-one confidential conversations between a trained and qualified personal coach and a client. In each conversation, the coach uses specific skills, tools, and techniques to help a client make powerful decisions and design motivated action in any area of life or business. These conversations can take place over a phone, video chat, a voice-message app, or in person.

Coaching conversations can look something like having a deep and meaningful private conversation with an intelligent best friend about one of your important life decisions, and that "best friend" is giving you 100% of their attention.

As a client, you might experience powerful change in your life within the first and the second conversation, or you may experience a series of small wins over several conversations that slowly add up to a profoundly new or a simply better place in life.

Sometimes, a coaching conversation focuses on what you learned about yourself when you didn't get the result you aimed for and how you may wish to adjust your plan for your next attempt.

Personal coaching is like your relationship with a personal trainer at the gym. In your relationship with a personal trainer, the trainer's focus is completely on you doing the work. You would not pay a personal trainer if they spent the entire session asking *you* to spot *them* or asking *you* to take pics of *them* for *their* socials. That's not what you pay a trainer for.

You pay a personal trainer to help you transform your physical body and health. Likewise, you pay a *personal coach* to challenge and stretch your goals in any area of life. A personal coach's sole focus in the conversation remains on your growth, your motivation, and your achievement.

While a personal trainer uses weights and equipment to build your muscles, a personal coach uses specific conversation tools and techniques to build clarity about what you truly want and ignite your deepest sense of motivation to take action.

You will learn many more details in the following chapters.

IS A COACH THE SAME AS A MENTOR OR THERAPIST?

No. While all three require one-on-one conversations, coaching involves a unique set of skills, techniques, and outcomes. Coaches help you make decisions in life or business by identifying and holding you accountable to your strengths, helping you envision what you genuinely want for your life or career, and assisting you in splitting apart the difference between your desires for your life and someone else's desire for your life.

Mentoring relies on someone else's insight or perspective, and therapy addresses and potentially diagnoses or labels past traumas and wounds. Forward-thinking, decision-making, and action-taking are essential to the coaching process, but those three elements are not required parts of a mentoring or therapy conversation.

Some mentors or therapists have undergone coaching qualifications and training, and so they may integrate a few skills and techniques into their mentoring or therapy. However, the entire process and the end results are very different when you have a dedicated personal coaching conversation. Therapy with an added spice of coaching is great, but metaphorically, it's radically different than an entire coaching gourmet meal - two very different processes, flavors, and results.

In the next chapter, I'll share more about the distinctions between coaching and therapy.

WHAT KIND OF RESULTS DO I GET FROM COACHING?

Coaches help you prioritize your desires for your life and business, establish a clear vision, make powerful decisions based on what motivates you the most, and help you to take action with inspiring accountability.

In some area of life, you might discover that you have been living according to someone else's desires that were never truly your own, and a coach helps you uncover that and discover your unique sense of purpose, passion, and direction that you may have forgotten or neglected.

Personal coaching helps you discover the knowledge you already have but have either forgotten, suppressed out of fear (whether you know it or not), or simply ignored because you're too busy.

A professional personal coach helps you think outside of any boxes where you may feel stuck and helps you identify an option that aligns most closely to your genuine motivations, goals, and values in life.

Results from coaching conversations have included mind-blowing accomplishments in medical health, physical fitness, career, business, financial health, having more fun, getting more rest, improving human relationships, expanding one's worldview, growing a healthy view of self, upgrading home or work environments, and having a healthier or more positive emotions and thought-life.

WHAT KIND OF PERSON BECOMES A COACH?

The more that a person has a natural sense of *optimism, intuition, and intelligence*, then the more likely that person is to be a powerfully effective personal coach.

Above all, a good personal coach is an optimistic type of person.

You'll meet coaches with all degrees of optimism, from realistic optimists to unrealistic optimists, people who are optimists in certain contexts to people who generally see the good in most things.

Hiring a pessimistic coach would be like going to a doctor who doesn't believe in medicine or treatment. That doctor would be out of business quite quickly and so would a pessimistic coach.

Although coaches are typically optimistic, one false assumption people tend to make is that coaches have their lives together 24/7, don't feel depressed, and feel endless motivation. That's simply an inhumane view. A coach is human with many human needs, not a machine.

No matter how many lives a brain surgeon saves, a brain surgeon can't do her own brain surgery. Rather, a surgeon needs a surgeon. In the same way, a coach also needs a coach. A personal coach is human, and when a coach loses motivation or loses sight of their own goals, they need to hire a coach to perform motivational surgery.

A psychologist needs a psychologist. A fireman caught in the midst of flames needs to be rescued. Likewise, every personal coach needs a personal coach.

A personal coach is naturally more inclined to enjoy encouraging people. A good coach enjoys listening and believes in the greatest potential of the human mind and heart.

Personal coaching also requires strong intuition, like a dancer feels the rhythm of a song. As a coach, I need to have a sense of where the rhythm of the conversation is going, while maintaining grace, spontaneity, and playful creativity. My movement depends on where you "move" in the conversation. As a coach, I need to take your direction, sense where you're going, and move with you.

If I have "two left feet" and can't sense your rhythm, I'll trip up the conversation and break our natural flow.

Although coaching relies heavily on optimism and intuition, a coach also needs intellect. A capacity for logic, analysis, and intelligent questioning are also key attributes of a great personal coach. That's because a coach needs to be able to think, reflect, pull apart arguments, recognize and call out your inconsistencies with passionate curiosity.

My background in philosophy prepared me for the depth and quality of questions I need to ask clients, and it helped me to identify theoretical fundamentals, such as the "Principles of Personal Change" that you will read later in this book.

ARE CREDENTIALS AND STANDARDS IMPORTANT?

If your money, time, quality of life, and decisions matter to you, then yes - credentials and standards are important.

Compared to the sciences of medicine and psychology, personal coaching is a newborn baby in the history of the world. It's a fairly new profession that has developed since the late 1990s and early 2000s.

Because this kind of coaching is so new, many people don't yet understand it. To make things more complicated, there are a few professional coaching organizations in the world, and each has their own slightly different definition of coaching.

The largest and most prestigious coaching organization in the world is called the International Coach Federation, otherwise known as the "ICF." It's an international establishment that sets standards of conduct, ethics, skills, credentialing, and accreditation in the field of professional coaching.

Organizations like the ICF are critical to setting quality standards in coaching.

Imagine if medical doctors weren't required by law to keep their equipment sterile. Imagine if your doctor wasn't required by law to keep your medical records private. Imagine if there were no laws around your doctor selling your personal information.

Laws around sterile equipment and medical privacy came about because a group of people demanded that we set a standard. Creating standards saves lives, time, and heartache.

Standardization creates higher quality services and safety, and laws are made to protect those standards. The medical world and even the many fields of psychology have set strict standards in many countries.

When it comes to personal coaching, finding coaches who have some form of standardized training is a much safer bet. Look for standards by looking for professional credentials. Unqualified coaches may influence your decisions about your life in unprofessional or even dangerous ways.

After receiving training from a few coach training programs, I decided to go for the most recognized qualifications I could earn in coaching at the time. So, I completed an ICF-accredited training program, exceeded the required client hours, completed required mentoring hours, took the three-hour exam, and then finally received my ICF credentials in 2015.

Now, with this book and theory - *The Science of Personal Coaching* - I hope to share some of those standards and set new ones.

EXERCISE (CHAPTER 1)

So, let's get started with your first exercise. This one might seem too simple, but it is designed to get you setup for future chapters.

Here are your first three points to earn.

EARN 1 POINT

1. Decide on the format of your diary to use for all of the exercises throughout this book. A notebook with paper and pen? A digital notepad? A document on your laptop? A cool smartphone app?

Earn your first point by picking a diary format, then opening up to your first blank page. Don't worry; earning points won't continue to be as simple as this first chapter.

EARN 1 POINT

2. Throughout this book, each exercise will ask you to write down the number of points you earned in its exercise. By the end of the book, if you have faithfully entered your points earned in each exercise, then you can easily add up all your points to calculate one final score.

So, now's the time to create the one official place in your diary where you will keep track of all of your points. Here's how to do it.

On the first blank page of your diary, write "Scoreboard" on the very top.

Underneath that, create two columns. On the top of the left column, write the title "Chapter Exercise Number" (or shorten it if you want to "Chpt. #" or similar), and then on the top of the right column, write the title "Points Earned."

Those two columns are what I will refer to as your "Scoreboard."

In the left column ("Chapter Exercise Number"), write down list the list of chapter numbers in this book, from Chapter 1 through to Chapter 21. There are a couple more chapters, but there are no exercises in them.

As you go through each chapter of this book and complete each exercise, use the second column ("Points Earned") to record the number of points you earned.

Your Scoreboard might look like the following sketch....

Scoreboard

Chapter Exercise Number	Points Earned
Chapter 1	——
Chapter 2	——
Chapter 3	——
Chapter 4	——
Chapter 5	——
Chapter 6	——
Chapter 7	——
Chapter 8	——
Chapter 9	——
Chapter 10	——
Chapter 11	——
Chapter 12	——
Chapter 13	——
Chapter 14	——
Chapter 15	——
Chapter 16	——
Chapter 17	——
Chapter 18	——
Chapter 19	——
Chapter 20	——
Chapter 21	——

Total Points ——————

EARN 1 POINT

3. Now, go to the next brand-new clean page in your diary, then write today's date and "Chapter 1" on the top.

Under that, write down your answer this question:

What are the top three reasons why you feel drawn to this book and to personal coaching in general?

To earn this point, honestly answer that question because it will help you remember why you're reading this book and doing these exercises.

MAXIMUM POINTS EARNED FOR THIS CHAPTER

You earn one point for each of the questions or challenges above, for a maximum of three points.

If you completed all three above, then you earned your first three points. If you only completed one or two, then you have earned a score of one or two.

Now, you can go to your Scoreboard in your Diary, and in the second column next to Chapter 1, write down the number of points you earned.

CHAPTER 2, HOW DO YOU DEFINE "PERSONAL COACHING"?

In the process of making it through a few coach training courses plus undergoing credentialing with the International Coach Federation (ICF) in 2015, I have heard several definitions of coaching.

The definitions I've seen are too vague and miss key components that distinguish it from similar professions.

So, with a professional background in communications and a love for coaching knowledge, I've attempted to answer the question, "How do you define *personal coaching*?"

Here are the short answer and the long answer.

THE SHORT ANSWER

To keep it simple, here's what I consider the best definition.

> personal coaching.
> *noun*
> *A series of one-on-one life-changing conversations that result in a client experiencing clarity and action*

THE LONG ANSWER

I carefully crafted the above definition after years of observation, analysis, and seeing what works. Here's why.

A series of...

In the definition of "personal coaching," I included the word "series" of conversations for an important reason. One of the key values of hiring a coach is the accountability — specifically, having follow-up conversations or a sequence of follow up conversations to report on your progress and reflect on your learning.

The accountability and expectation to report back to your coach on what happened helps you get clarity, helps you receive validation and encouragement where needed, and then supports you as you design a next step of action that is aligns with your unique values and motivations.

There is often a surprising sense of motivation to get things done when you know that you're going to talk to your coach the next day or in a couple days or next week. That kind of accountability has a way of keeping you on your toes and moving forward. So, a "series" of conversations is key.

To use the personal trainer metaphor, you will not experience significant results after only one session of weightlifting with a personal trainer. Rather, you begin to see results over a series of sessions - coming back again and again to your coach for more growth and forward movement.

One-on-one...

Personal coaching is one-on-one, as opposed to group coaching which is one-on-many.

Personal coaching looks at the whole person in a confidential way, directly thinking out loud and discussing your unique desires, values, wins, and motivations. It offers the luxury of individual focus with a sense of privacy and safety that often comes with one person whose 100% attention is on you, undivided.

Life-changing conversations...

Most natural human conversations are a give-and-take situation in which two people each explore the needs, wants, or opinions of the other person to varying degrees. However, 100% of the focus of a *personal coaching conversation* aims for the client's clarity on what they want and a motivated next step to get it.

A professional coach is paid for keeping you, as client, on the path of a meaningful and effective conversation that is fully focused on changing your life - not to shoot the breeze or small talk about the weather.

And by "life-changing," someone may be tempted to think that something life-changing is unrelated to work. However, when I say life-changing, I mean that coaching can focus on any and all areas of your precious life, including your work-life, office-life, social-life at work, and anything having to do with what you do at work, because work is where you spend the majority of your adult life.

That result in a client experiencing clarity and action.

If clarity and action don't happen, then neither has coaching happened.

A *personal coaching conversation* remains focused on only two outcomes and in this order: (1) the client's vision for what they want or genuinely desire, which I call "clarity" and (2) the most motivating next step that the client would like to take, which I call "action."

The word "client" also implies that this is a professional relationship between two people, where one is paying for a service and results.

WHAT ARE THE DISTINCTIONS BETWEEN THERAPY AND PERSONAL COACHING?

One of the other ways to understand personal coaching is to know at least a basic summary of the professional field it was born from and what may have changed since.

For most of its history, the study of psychology has focused heavily on identifying and examining disorders. Since the late 1990s, however, pioneers in the science of mental health have created a branch of research that identifies and studies human strengths and values rather than disorders. This field of study is now formally called "positive psychology." The profession of coaching grew out of positive psychology.

Because coaching grew out of the study of psychology, there are many common characteristics between coaching and therapy. That relationship can leave people confused, to some degree, about the line between personal coaches and therapist-related professions such as psychotherapists, psychologists, or counsellors. However, those of us who earned ICF credentials are obligated to draw some clear distinctions.

Here are what I recognize as the greatest distinctions.

Distinction 1: Commitment to Change

There are three major differences between the conversation a coach has with a client versus the conversation that a therapist - or other mental health professional - has with a client.

I once heard a therapist say that his clients "are people who felt they had no strength to change their lives." And that's a beautiful service - to offer a space where people can think out loud without a requirement to change. In contrast, as a coach, I serve people who know they're tolerating something for too long and are ready to change.

A strong desire and commitment to change is an essential part of the coaching process, but it is not a requirement for therapy.

Therapy clients are generally free to participate in therapy without a strong drive to change their lives, but coaching clients know that there is at least one area they are committed to - and able to - change. I haven't yet met a qualified coach who wouldn't first check your commitment to change before starting the coaching relationship.

While traditional therapists might help you identify problems in your past or childhood, personal coaches take a contrasting approach by helping you identify opportunities for your future.

I go to a therapist for insight, when I need a diagnosis or analysis of a problem, or when I need professional mental health advice. On the other hand, I go to a professional personal coach when I am ready and willing to identify a new direction or make a change in my life, career, or business, and then have accountability throughout the day or week.

I go to a professional personal coach when I need clarity about a new or improved direction in life and a clearer vision.

Distinction 2: Commitment to Action

According to the International Coach Federation's (ICF) list of required skills, or the "11 Core Competencies" as they have been called,[11] a coach must demonstrate the ability to help clients design action and make actionable progress. Four of those required coaching skills are:

- designing action,
- planning and goal setting,
- creating awareness of these actions, and
- managing progress and accountability.

Action is a powerful distinction of coaching. When following the ICF's 11 Core Competencies, a coaching conversation does not end with reflection or introspection as many therapy appointments do; rather, it requires a motivated action.

The action that comes out of a coaching conversation can be anything at all, from setting aside time to reflect further, to making a high-stakes business deal or asking a long-term partner to get married. Big or small, any action matters.

To take action means to convert your dreams or wishful thinking onto actual plans on the calendar. Dreams become goals only when they have a commitment to action. Otherwise, they're only dreams.

Distinction 3: Legality

The third distinction of personal coaching from mental health professions is legality.

As I mention elsewhere in this book, the practice of therapy-related professions is strictly regulated by many governments. In contrast, because it is a fairly new field of study and practice in human history, most governments have not passed laws that directly regulate coaching.

Regulations happen over time. For example, in the early days of medicine, there was very little government regulation of doctors.

Imagine a time when surgeons were not expected to meet any legal standards. Some doctors may wash their hands between procedures, but others could go straight from doing a postmortem to open-heart surgery. No regulations around sterilization meant serious medical danger, high mortality rates, and plenty of opportunity for unethical behavior.

In response over time, people came together to create national organizations to develop standards. Once it became time to create new legislation, governments consulted with those organizations to develop national legal regulations. Now medical doctors have far more strict requirements in order to maintain their practice and protect patients.

When it comes to coaching, the ICF is the largest coaching organization in the world today, and its members are in the long process of creating coaching standards around the world.

I've heard it said that when coaching laws are introduced, the ICF will most likely be the organization of authority that governments consult. That's why I stuck with the ICF and will refer to its standards throughout this training program.

HOW DO OTHERS DEFINE COACHING?

As part of my credentialing process with the International Coaching Federation ("ICF"), I learned their definition of coaching: "Partnering with clients in a thought-provoking and creative process that inspires them to maximize their personal and professional potential."[2]

I agree with the ICF's definition in spirit, but I found the language too vague.

The language of "thought-provoking and creative process" leaves room for confusion on what the word "process" actually means. What's the name and order of steps of this "process" that they are talking about? I earned my credentials through them, and I did not see a process that I could follow step by step to guide me through a coaching conversation. Principles and skills were presented - yes, but a repeatable system or chronological order of steps to make each conversation easier? No.

The essential word missing there in ICF's definition is "conversation," and that's why I designed a more specific definition and put that word into it. The *process* is a conversation.

Also, the coaching conversation does not only "inspire them to maximize their personal and professional potential." Coaching does far above and beyond potential. The ICF specifically requires clients to have action plans and accountability to those actions, and so that key word - action - is also in my definition.

"Action" is such an essential part of coaching that it's included in about 30% of the basic coaching skills required by the ICF.

So, with all of that being the case, I've taken ICF's high level definition and made it more practical, so that it points to the measurable events that make coaching a success - clarity, action, and series of conversations.

Personal coaching is "a series of one-on-one life-changing conversations that result in a client experiencing clarity and action."

To know more about how coaching is practiced throughout the world, check out Chapter 22 in this book, titled "Coaching Worldwide." There you'll find fascinating research on how coaching is practiced throughout the world.

Ok, now that logistics are out of the way, it's time to start focusing on the topic of *you*... or at least my assumptions about you. That's what we'll look at in the next chapter.

EXERCISE (CHAPTER 2)

In your diary, write today's date and "Chapter 2" on top of the page.

EARN 1 POINT

1. Think about some area of your life that you would like to change right now.

Then, imagine that you have in your hand a magic wand that guarantees you will gain 100% clarity about that area of your life, and it also guarantees that any action you take will be successful.

So, what area of life would you use your magic wand to change?

This light-hearted question is intended to help you sense the wonder of getting clarity and taking action.

EARN 1 POINT

2. After reading these first few chapters, how do you see yourself using this book - to learn a professional level of coaching or to learn casually for fun or general interest, or something else?

EARN 1 POINT

3. From your personal perspective, what do you see as the most important difference between a professional therapist and a professional personal coach?

MAXIMUM POINTS EARNED FOR THIS CHAPTER

You earn 1 point for answering each of the questions above for a maximum of 3 points.

Count the number of points you completed and write down the total number on your Scoreboard, as described in Exercise Chapter 1.

CHAPTER 3, WHAT DO I ASSUME ABOUT YOU?

Now that you have a better understanding of the background and general logistics of personal coaching, we can start focusing on you. Yes, you.

For many of these exercises, I'll show you how coaching works, but I'll also *coach you* at the same time. So, in many parts of this book, I'll speak to you directly as my "client" and not only as a coach in training.

Why? Because, if you want to learn the power of coaching, the formal process "sticks" better when you experience its power as a client.

So, think of the upcoming exercises as a series of coaching conversations with me.

Of course, having a verbal conversation with me versus reading a book that I've written are two completely different experiences. A verbal coaching conversation has an emotional and motivational depth that a book may never have. Still, this book's exercises are designed in such a way to stir your emotions, as if we were talking live.

Before we get started, I'll begin by setting expectations. In other words, I'll be sharing five assumptions I have about you as my client. If you decide to become a coach, you can also take these five assumptions with you into your relationships with *your* clients.

WHAT ARE MY FIVE ASSUMPTIONS?

Doctors assume their patients visit their office because they want to get well. Lawyers assume their clients hire them because they need legal assistance with a matter that they can't handle on their own. Sports coaches assume their teams want someone to help them win.

In each of those examples, there are basic assumptions that each professional has when you walk in their door. Additional layers of assumptions follow those, depending on the profession. Likewise, as your personal coach, I have a few assumptions about you.

During our first coaching conversation, I like to explicitly tell you about these assumptions to make sure that we both agree on the basics of our coaching relationship.

Assumption 1: Knowledge

You already know the answers to the questions you have about your own life.

Whenever you don't think you have an answer, the answer is your search. In other words, when you don't think that you have an answer, the answer is to find your next step to obtain the answer.

 It's like the saying, "You are the expert of you."

In other words, you, as the client, have the answers about your life and what is healthy or right for you to do next.

Other people may have opinions or even insights about you, but only you can sense what your conscience is saying. Only you can fully feel your own feelings. Only you can think your original thoughts. Only you can see the images as they appear in your mind.

Assumption 2: Resources

You have the resources you need to search for your answers.

It may involve searching the internet, asking other people, hiring an expert, going back to school, meditating, exploring a spiritual path, or some other creative way of finding what you need; but you have the resources for starting your journey right now.

When you don't have the physical resources, then I trust that you have the emotional or mental resources to begin the creative search for the people or places or things that lead you to your answer.

Assumption 3: Honesty

I trust that you are honest when you say you feel ready to make a change in your life.

This is a prerequisite for all personal coaching - to feel ready and committed to make a change, whether you think the needed change is large or small.

A willingness to change can express itself in many forms. Paying for coaching services or buying a book like this are both honest expressions and evidence that you're ready to take action and make change happen.

I believe you will be honest with me about what kind of change you genuinely wish to make, and when I challenge you on that, I believe you will give me an honest reply.

Assumption 4: False Assumptions

You have possibly made unchallenged assumptions throughout life about yourself and the world that, when challenged by me, might prove to be false.

I'm going to help you recognize and clear out those assumptions that are getting in the way of your goals.

Assumption 5: Emotional Ends

For every physical, tangible, or material goal you have, you're also seeking an emotional end. In other words, you may say that you'd like a new career, a new relationship, a new this or new that, and while I will help you get there, I also recognize that your end objective is to feel an emotion behind it.

Maybe you think your goal is to change careers, but you also have an emotional end - either to feel peace or excitement or satisfaction.

Maybe you think your goal is to establish a new intimate relationship, but you also have an emotional end - either to feel adrenaline or attraction or joy or comfort.

Maybe you think your goal is to invest in or purchase something, but you also have an emotional end - to feel novelty or excitement or a feeling of being rewarded.

And that is the wonder of life - to feel. What's the point of achieving anything if we feel nothing emotionally when we achieve it?

On the other hand, sometimes the deeper reason or purpose behind your goal is to *avoid an emotion* - to *no longer* feel confused, to *escape* sadness, or to *distract yourself from* another negative feeling that's weighing you down.

When you want to make a change, there are material reasons that appear on the surface; but, on a deeper level, I believe that it's an emotional state that is the end goal beyond the physical world achievement. You want it in your hands because it will make you feel something.

The key to understanding this is that your options open up widely, and you discover that there are many ways to reach that same emotional state, or even far better.

EXERCISE (CHAPTER 3)

In your diary, write today's date and "Chapter 3" on top of the page.

Under that, answer each of the following questions the best you can in a way that's meaningful to you. You only need one sentence or two for each.

EARN 1 POINT

1. Think of one specific situation in your life right now that you have a desire to change, and then answer all of the following questions about that situation. Here's the first:

What is at least one positive or encouraging fact about your *current* state or *current* situation that you know deep down inside of yourself?

EARN 1 POINT

2. Regarding the above situation, what is one resource (either a person or a thing) that can potentially help you find the answers you need?

EARN 1 POINT

3. How honest are you with yourself about the amount of desire you have in you right now to make change happen in this situation?

EARN 1 POINT

4. What are one or two false assumptions that you might be making about this situation?

EARN 1 POINT

5. What emotion or emotions do you imagine yourself feeling after you successfully make the change?

MAXIMUM POINTS EARNED FOR THIS CHAPTER

You earn 1 point for answering each of the questions above for a maximum of 5 points.

This has been an exploration of the five assumptions introduced in this chapter.

Count the number of points you completed and write down the total number on your Scoreboard, as described in Exercise Chapter 1.

EXERCISE (CHAPTER 3)
The Science of Personal Coaching

CHAPTER 4, THE 20 PRINCIPLES OF PERSONAL CHANGE

WHERE DID THESE 20 PRINCIPLES COME FROM?

In her TED Talk, "The Gift and Power of Emotional Courage," award-winning Harvard Medical School psychologist Susan David PhD said, "research now shows that the radical acceptance of all of our emotions, even the messy and difficult ones, is the cornerstone to resilience, thriving, and true, authentic happiness."[3]

If you had no emotional obstacles, then personal growth or change would be easy. But whenever we talk about change, we're talking about the emotional challenges and obstacles that come with it.

The emotions involved in the process of change are often the "messy and difficult" kind that Dr. David mentioned above. But she makes the answer sound so easy - just "radically accept" them.

Ok, but how?

As you work toward your destinations in life and go through the growth and change that they require, how do you accept the emotional storms along the way?

One of the most powerful ways to do this, as I discovered through coaching, is to have a clear vision or, in other words, set clear expectations of the *emotional cost* of your destination or goal.

When you know what travelling the road ahead is going to cost emotionally, you can better prepare for the trip.

WILL YOU COUNT THE COST?

So, I designed these 20 Principles of Personal Change, to help you understand and budget your emotional costs ahead of time. These are based on my observations and my own transformation experience as a coach and a client.

I could have created a smaller and more marketable list to make it sound easier, but removing any of these would be like removing rungs from your ladder; it will make the climb much harder and more dangerous for you.

There are many principles because there are many challenges ahead for you, but if you meditate on these 20 Principles, it can help you set clear and sober expectations, helping you climb the ladder with more certainty and emotional resilience toward your goal.

As your coach, it's my job to believe these principles and help you apply them to your goals. They help me challenge you to prepare and accept the emotional cost to make change happen.

THE 20 PRINCIPLES

#1. Sustainable personal change will happen in proportion to the strength of my desire for it to happen.

#2. Sometimes, I must first reach a point of feeling completely fed-up with something before I can find enough desire to fuel the change that needs to happen.

#3. Material resources are not an obstacle for me as people with the least number of resources have achieved world-changing progress because their desire found a way.

#4. It's not a question of *if I can* do something, but, rather, a question of *how much it will cost* emotionally, physically, materially, and financially to get it.

#5. It is equally important to ask myself how much it will cost *not to do it*.

#6. Healthy personal change happens when I am both honest and compassionate with myself at the same time and in *equal* amounts.

#7. When I make decisions based on *someone else's* convictions or values that *conflict with my own*, I lose some degree of integrity and power.

#8. I do not control or force attitudes on other people, but I can persuade, influence, or model the right attitude for them.

#9. I am 100% responsible for the attitude I choose in *every* situation.

#10. Regularly rewarding myself and acknowledging the smallest evidence of my progress is important because it has the power to create positive mental momentum.

#11. Accountability changes behavior and choices.

#12. When I say a word, everyone has slightly different pictures in their minds than I do. For that reason, it's better to communicate with imagery, metaphors, and visuals whenever possible so that we have a better change of agreement and understanding.

#13. When I maintain a victim-mentality, I oppose my own success and progress.

#14. As I journey toward my goal, it's healthy to give myself time and space to slow down to heal after experiencing heavy or painful emotions.

#15. When life gives me the four-letter word that starts with "s-h," it's my job to consider it fertilizer and see what life I can grow from it.

#16. The language or words that I choose to frame my situation matters.

#17. Knowing what I *don't want* is important, but I can become easily "stuck" in a negative cycle if I don't identify what it is that *I do want*.

#18. I am often wiser than I believe myself to be.

#19. Without identifying and nurturing *my own vision* for my life, I end up living according to someone else's vision by default.

#20. I don't make "mistakes"; rather I understand them as learning opportunities to make my next attempt smarter and better-informed, and the only "mistake" I can make is to refuse to learn from an experience.

EXERCISE (CHAPTER 4)

In your diary, write today's date and "Chapter 4" on top of the page.

EARN UP TO 20 POINTS

For each of the 20 principles, write down one inspiring or positive example from your life or the life of someone you know. Each one of your examples can be very big or very small.

Whether it's an example from your life or someone else's, identify specifically the action or decision in which you see the principle illustrated.

You can think back to a time in your life long ago or you can think to recent times. If the example is from the life of someone you know personally or someone you have heard of, then it can be from any time in that person's history.

Keep your answers as short and simple as possible - only one or two sentences for each principle.

Most importantly, this exercise aims to be a reflection on stories that inspire you – i.e., what makes you feel positive or wise. So only write down what makes you feel good. The examples of each principle can be large or small. It's ok if they are itsy-bitsy-teenie-weenie-tiny examples.

MAXIMUM POINTS EARNED FOR THIS CHAPTER

You earn 1 point for each of the principles that you provide an example of, for a maximum of 20 points.

Count the number of points you completed and write down the total number on your Scoreboard, as described in Exercise Chapter 1.

CHAPTER 5, YOUR MOTIVATORS

As your coach, I ask questions to uncover your motivations behind your goals.

One of the many kinds of questions around your motivations might be, "Whose values are you working toward?"

Are you working hard to align your decisions with what genuinely motivates you or are you working hard to align with someone else's motivations while neglecting your own? When everyone's motivations complement or agree with each other, then it makes for a beautiful story of helping each other live out their purpose.

However, many people are living the values of a family member, a boss, or someone else, while at the same time secretly feeling a sense of meaningless.

And while supporting someone else's motivations sounds like it can be "the right thing," it might quickly become "the wrong thing" if it means that your deeper sense of values or motivations are neglected or that your conscience is seared in the process.

Becoming aware of what uniquely motivates *you* can help you quickly resolve the sense of meaningless that comes with "living someone else's life."

When everyone can identify and then make decisions according to their known motivators, everyone's work becomes more lively, aligned, and productive.

The idea of "motivators" is to identify what uniquely motivates you so that you can make decisions that better align with your sense of meaning and purpose. In this chapter, we will identify yours.

THE RESEARCH BEHIND YOUR MOTIVATORS

The idea of "motivators" that I'm about to introduce is birthed from psychological theory and research.

I am most inspired by a reputable research project called the *VIA Classification of Strengths* conducted by the University of Pennsylvania and the VIA Institute on Character.[4] This brilliant team of 55 social scientists, led by Christopher Peterson PhD, came up with a list of what is called "character strengths and virtues." This list is an important tool used globally by coaches to help their clients align decisions with what uniquely and truly motivates them.

The VIA Classification of Strengths is only one of several inspiring studies that demonstrate the importance of identifying what truly motivates you and how important it is for your well-being to consciously make decisions that align with your unique motivations.

There is also Shalom H. Schwartz, a psychologist and researcher, who developed the Theory of Basic Human Values. His research shows that people experience greater well-being when they act in ways that align with their core values.

Separate work from psychologists Edward Deci and Richard Ryan shows that when people make decisions based on their inherent motivations, they will have greater psychological well-being.

Wherever I talk about motivators, I repeat the same message: a disconnect between your decisions and your values or "motivators," as I call them, can have a negative impact on everything.

Motivators are life-giving. Your individual motivators keep you committed to a project or person when it becomes hard work. They are an essential tool for whole-hearted and life-changing decision-making.

HOW TO IDENTIFY YOUR PERSONAL MOTIVATORS

As humans, first we week to survive; then, we seek to thrive. In other words, we first look to establish safety (surviving), so that we can then build meaningfully upon it (thriving).

Even though they have access to plenty of food, water, and the basics, many people feel a sense of something emotionally missing. And in those situations, what they may be lacking is taking the big step from a life of *surviving* to a life of building a future that is personally or emotionally meaningful.

Your motivators are the steppingstones that have the power to take you from "just getting by" to the kind of future-building that feels meaningful. It starts with identifying exactly *what motivates you individually* and then making decisions *based on that value*.

We don't necessarily make decisions based on our own personal values. An eye-opening study found that we are more likely to make decisions based on our own values when we are conscious of those values.[5]

If you don't identify your values, put a name to them, and have them in your mind when making a decision, then your unique values may not play the role that you need them to. The risk is that key decisions in your life might potentially have little to do with what you *actually value the most*.

No wonder people make decisions they regret on a regular basis!

So far, I've used the word "values," but from now on I'm going to more often call them "motivators." That's because "motivators" is a word that more accurately gets to the heart of what "values" do. Our values are our motivators.

Motivators make life and work feel meaningful, giving us the fuel to do and be the best we can. They reveal the shape of who we are so that we can find where we fit in this world.

Personal coaches make you conscious of your motivators, as you make decisions in the coaching conversation. When you have your first coaching "conversation" with me in the next chapter, you will know your motivators and will be able to integrate them to make more powerful and meaningful decisions.

I can't stress this enough, uncovering your motivators is one of the most important discoveries I can make about you as your coach. If I know your motivators, then I have an effective tool to keep you authentic to yourself and more committed to the decisions you make during coaching. It's like knowing the player's best moves before the game.

Identifying and using your key motivators in day-to-day decision-making may be the easiest and most powerful way to change your life.

Ok, but how do I use motivators in a practical way? When you have a decision to make about your career, relationships, money, time, health, personal growth, or attitude, simply ask yourself, "Which option best aligns with my motivators?"

It's that easy. The hardest part is *remembering to ask yourself* that question, but that's what I'm here for you as your coach.

THE 10 MOTIVATORS

Inspired by research that I shared earlier, I put together the following list. Here is a list of the 10 motivators, along with some words in brackets to help you further understand what each one means.

- Courage (bravery, facing external or internal opposition, provocation, challenge)
- Creativity (ingenuity, change, open-mindedness, innovation, invention, novelty)
- Beauty (the visual, audible, emotional, artistic, or spiritual attractiveness of people or things)
- Health (wholeness, energy, vitality, physical and mental well-being, self-care)
- Wisdom and Knowledge (curiosity, learning, making sense of how the world works)
- Community (society as a whole, empathy, love of people, teamwork)
- Justice (individual or community rights, fairness, equality, citizenship, integrity)
- Order (organization, control, prioritization, structure, self-regulation)
- Transcendence (gratitude, laughter, hope, optimism, humor, humility, spirituality)
- Freedom (light-heartedness, unrestraint, flexibility, liberation, opportunity)

In this chapter's exercise, you'll find out which one or two are *yours*.

EXERCISE (CHAPTER 5)

In your diary, write today's date and "Chapter 5" on top of the page.

To complete this exercise, find a place where you feel safe and comfortable for a few minutes. Most importantly, hide yourself away from interruptions so that you can pay close attention to your inner dialogue and emotional state.

Now, we're going to have a little bit of fun with a coaching exercise that has practical and powerful results. Here it is!

It's a bit like a game of "make believe."

Imagine yourself being able to create a brand-new world. This whole new world is yours alone to create, and you make all the rules! Based on that, here are a few questions.

EARN 1 POINT

1. Out of the list of ten motivators that you read at the end of this chapter, you can only take *one of the ten* motivators with you to start your new world. Which one would you take?

Write down your answer in your diary.

EARN 1 POINT

2. Now imagine that one year has passed since starting your brand-new world. You're now able to invite a *second* motivator. Which one would you take?

Write the second motivator in your diary.

EARN 1 POINT

3. It's quite simple, but profound. You've just uncovered the secret to making meaningful decisions in your life that best align with who you are. Now, when you find yourself at any crossroad, you can ask yourself, "What aligns best with [insert your first motivator]?"

And if you still feel stuck, ask yourself, "What aligns best with [insert your second motivator]?"

To earn your third point in this exercise, it's time to put your motivator to work.

We humans make thousands of decisions each day, so certainly you are going to make either some big or small decisions over the next 24 hours. To earn this point, pick one decision you're going to make in the next 24 hours.

It might be a decision around what to do with your time, what to eat, what to say to someone or how to say it, what time to go to bed, or how you are going to celebrate something.

In two or three sentences, describe how can you incorporate your first motivator into that decision? It can be any decision. Simply pick one, and then briefly describe how you will integrate your motivator into your decision-making process.

MAXIMUM POINTS EARNED FOR THIS CHAPTER

You earn 1 point for answering each of the questions above for a maximum of 3 points.

Count the number of points you completed and write down the total number on your Scoreboard, as described in Exercise Chapter 1.

CHAPTER 6, YOUR FIRST COACHING CONVERSATION

ARE YOU READY?

Before I even schedule the first conversation with you, I'd start by confirming whether there's something in your life that you want to change and how important it is for you to change it.

You can bring a horse to water, but you can't force it to drink - there's no sense in moving forward with someone who has little or no desire to change.

But you're not a horse being dragged to the water. The fact that you're reading this book right now is an indication that you're ready to make a change in some area of your life or career. That's where all coaching relationships begin - a desire strong enough to make change happen.

On a scale from 0 to 10, if you have a desire of anywhere from 8 to 10 to make a change in your life in any area, then you're ready for a coaching conversation.

When someone has a score of 7 or below, it's highly likely that coaching will not be effective at this time of their life. A person may be content with their life as-is, in which case they have no desire to change, and that's often a great place to be in life.

On the other hand, a person may be dissatisfied with their life but they're happier suffering until the dissatisfaction turns to intolerable pain. And other times, a person may want to change something in their life, but they don't yet have enough desire just yet.

So, now that I know you want to be here, this chapter will cover our first formal coaching "conversation."

SHALL WE SEE IF WE'RE ON THE SAME PAGE?

Before we get personal and start working on getting clarity, there are a several professional standards that the International Coach Federation (ICF) requires their credentialed coaches to demonstrate. Failure to observe these potentially can result in a coach losing their credentials.

Among those standards that are most relevant to kicking off the coaching relationship, two of them are "Meeting Ethical Guidelines and Professional Standards" and "Establishing The Coaching Agreement."

Meeting Ethical Guidelines and Professional Standards

Normally, to ensure that we are on the same page regarding ethics and standards, I would ask that you sign a contract to confirm your understanding of what coaching is and isn't as well as our professional boundaries, or I would present you an electronic agreement to a documented terms of service.

However, coaching is so new that many people don't understand it enough to sign a contract right away or commit to anything longer term. They might want to experience it first.

It is okay to have a first conversation without a formal signed contract, but in that case, I would still be required to establish an agreement verbally with you at the beginning of or before the very first conversation to touch on any of the contract topics that you don't yet know.

Then, after the first conversation and only if you decide to continue, I could introduce a formal contract document or terms and conditions.

Contents of a proper agreement, such as confidentiality, avoiding conflicts of interest, and other ethical guidelines can be found on coachingfederation.org. I'll also introduce key content in the next section.

Establishing the Coaching Agreement

What do you agree to as a coaching client?

At the time of writing the third edition of this book, the ICF offers a sample professional coaching contract that you can find on their site (coachingfederation.org). In that sample, you will find exactly what you're agreeing to as a coaching client, plus the standard legal sections you would find in any professional services contract, such as termination of the agreement, severability, liability, applicable law, and binding effect. It also includes essential information about the ethical behavior coaches are obligated to follow.

Below is the list of what contract topics I would cover *verbally* at the beginning of or prior to our first conversation, and I've turned each of them into questions.

It might take 10 to 15 minutes or more to get through all of it on a live call, but the good news is that the entire list of topics to cover - except for "time frame" - only needs to be covered verbally in the very first conversation, and then it belongs in a written or documented contract when the client agrees to pay for services.

You'll also see most of the following in Chapter 23's Destination Conversation Checklist, in the first gear section of course.

Time frame

I confirm the time frame that we agreed to for today so that I can drive the conversation at the right speed, ensuring we complete all stages on time.

"You booked 90 minutes. Would you like to keep that as our time frame today?"

Client-centricity

I remind you that the conversation will center around you and the direction you want to go - not on me or my wishes or anyone else's.

"I will keep the conversation focused on you. If the conversation ever shifts toward me and how I'm feeling or thinking, or how anyone else feels or thinks, I'll shift the conversation back over to how you are feeling or thinking. How does that sound to you?"

Cancellations, lateness, and rescheduling

I ask if you have any questions about the cancellation, lateness, and rescheduling.

"How much do you understand about cancellations, lateness, and rescheduling?"

Coaching definition

I ask if you understood what coaching sets out to do.

"How much would you like to know right now about the definition of coaching — what it is and what it's not?"

Confidentiality

I confirm you understand that everything you and I discuss will remain strictly confidential and it is my duty to keep the conversation confidential. The only exception would be if a court subpoenas my records or if I feel that someone is in danger.

"I'm obligated to keep everything from our conversation strictly confidential. What, if any, questions or concerns do you have about confidentiality?"

Permission

I let you know that everything we touch on in our conversation is by your permission and at your discretion, such as the direction of our conversation and your willingness to answer my questions.

"The direction of our conversation, the topics, and my questions are all going to happen only with your permission. At any point, if you feel that I'm going in a direction without your permission, how do you feel about stopping to let me know?"

"Also, if I notice that our conversation is heading away from your goal for the conversation, I may interrupt the conversation to bring that to your attention. Then I can check if you would like to continue down that road or get back to your expressed purpose of the call. How do you feel about that?"

Notes

Part of the coaching process requires me to take notes while the client is speaking, so that I can remember their key words and phrases in order to keep them accountable.

"So that I remember important key words and phrases in our conversation, I'd like to take notes and of course keep them confidential. While taking notes, you might hear me pause to write or type. Do I have your permission to take notes?"

Regularly scheduled conversations

I will let you know that the power of coaching requires a series of conversations in which each conversation follows up on the previous conversation. So, it is essential to understand coaching results depend on a regular schedule of some sort and a commitment to show up.

A dream that isn't on the calendar remains only a dream; so, I'm here to help you turn your dreams into real life events that go on the calendar.

"Significant coaching results depend on a series of regularly scheduled conversations, not one only. If we decided to have regular conversations, how would you imagine fitting coaching conversations into your schedule – short and frequent conversations (e.g. 10 to 15 minutes a day) or longer and less frequent (e.g. 45 to 60 minutes a week)?"

Communication technology options

I remind you of all the communication options we have over the internet, help you understand how to use them if needed, and discuss what to do if there are any interruptions in our connection.

"What communication technologies or apps do you like the most or which ones would you like to try for future conversations?"

The Five Assumptions

I bring up assumptions I have about you and every client, but this will depend on how much you already know about coaching.

"In each conversation, I come to the conversation with a few beliefs about you and your capability. Would you like to hear them?"

Your decisions

I remind you that coaching is not mentoring, counselling, or advising, so I do not make any decisions for you or push you in any direction, but I am here to help you keep accountable to your own sense of self and your unique motivations in those decisions.

"Coaching will not involve my opinion or me telling you what to do; instead, my role is to challenge you to make your own decisions that keep you true to yourself, that move you forward with your goals, and that align with your unique motivations."

Availability and responsiveness

Here is where I set the stage on what you can expect in regard to which ways you can reach me such as which communication tools I use, when I'm available, how to book a conversation ahead of time, and a time expectation for responding to your messages.

"These are the apps where you can reach me.... The main app we agreed to use is.... This is the way to book in a conversation anytime.... The days and times that I am available are .... You'll know when I have a day off because I'll let you know by.... Whenever you send me a message on the app, you can expect a response within a time frame of anywhere from right away and up to...."

Questions

I ask if you need help understanding anything we've just discussed.

"Thanks for your patience. I shouldn't ever need to take up that much time of our conversation time again, now that we've covered all of that. So, before we start focusing on you and your goals, what, if any, questions do you have for me?"

Those are the basics to cover, but only for the first conversation. Now, when it's your turn to coach someone, you'll have everything you need to get started with them in an ethical, professional way.

Now that we've gotten that out of the way, let's get down to business. Your business. Your life.

OUR FIRST CONVERSATION

Reading a book is a very different experience when compared to a live coaching conversation, but I have first-hand experience of a book powerfully changing lives. So, I know that working on these exercises through this book has strong potential.

Chapter 6's Exercise gives you a series of questions and answers that serve as "our first coaching conversation."

Our Chapter 6 "conversation" could take about an hour or more because of the depth of its questions. It will require you to pause, think, feel, and then answer. So, if needed, remember that you can break up your hour into separate, shorter, and dedicated sessions.

Your honest answers will lay the foundation for your success in this book. To answer the questions with heartfelt sincerity, schedule a time when you can lock yourself away from distractions. This might mean simply hanging a *Do Not Disturb* sign on your door, or it might mean cuddling up in the corner of a cafe by yourself with a coffee and a pair of headphones.

Now, it's time to get to know yourself better and identify your current needs and desires.

I suggest that you wait to read Chapter 6's Exercise until you are sitting down, ready and relaxed somewhere with plenty of time to concentrate - allowing yourself around one hour might be safe.

As a reminder, remember to take your diary with you so that you have one place for all of your answers and your history of points.

EXERCISE (CHAPTER 6)

In your diary, write today's date and "Chapter 6" on top of the page.

Welcome to our first coaching conversation! While I can't hear you say anything in reply, I just want to give you a warm smile and say that I'm so grateful you're here.

I call this very first conversation your "Destination Conversation," which is a term that we'll look into further in the next chapter; however, to put it simply, a *destination* is a worthy long-term goal of yours that we will uncover together.

We discover what destination you want to drive toward in our very first coaching conversation. Since the last section of this chapter already covered the logistics and essentials about our agreement, I can skip those kinds of questions here and get straight to the important topics.

You might need one uninterrupted hour to go through this.

Take your time and carefully answer each question in your diary.

If you feel unsure about what a question means, simply choose a meaning that makes the most sense to *you*.

For each question, write down *both* the question (or a shortened version of the question) and your heartfelt answer.

EARN 1 POINT

1. What do you hope to get out of this exercise?

EARN 1 POINT

2. How much time do you have right now to spend on this exercise?

EARN 1 POINT

3. Do you feel like you're in a safe space right now, relaxed and comfortable with no interruptions or distractions?

If your answer is no, what can you do right now to ensure you work on this exercise in a more comfortable environment?

EARN 1 POINT

4. Tell me about either one of the happiest or one of funniest moments of your life — just a short story of a couple sentences. Pick your favorite memory from long ago or recent times.

EARN 1 POINT

5. Tolerating something means that you're putting up with or allowing something in your life, even though you recognize that something about it isn't right for you.

What are the top three things you are currently tolerating?

EARN 1 POINT

6. Now, let's take a look at your life overall. For each of the areas listed below, write down a score of one through ten (1-10) to describe how satisfied you feel about that area of your life. A score of 1 means that it couldn't be any worse, and a score of 10 means it couldn't be any better.
A. Body health (including medical health and fitness)
B. Financial health
C. Restful activities (low energy downtime, reclining, relaxing, chillout activities)
D. Playful activities (having fun, energizing activities, celebrating - whether big or small).
E. Emotions and thought life
F. Occupation (career, trade, or business)
G. Discovery (learning, novelty, and exploration)
H. Time management (prioritization, scheduling, and calendar
I. Self-view (how you view yourself and self-esteem)
J. Worldview (spiritual, religious, intellectual, moral, or philosophical life)
K. Environments at work, home, and anywhere in between (lighting, furniture, space, noise, etc.)
L. Human relationships (including friendship, intimate partnership, family, professional, political, or any other)

EARN 1 POINT

7. In Chapter 5's Exercise, you discovered your top two motivators.
At this time in your life, in what ways can you imagine aligning your life decisions more closely with your motivators?

EARN 1 POINT

8. It's make-believe time.

Using your imagination, make believe that it's now *one year from today*, and you have successfully made a significant change in your life. You're deeply satisfied or relieved that you made this change.

If you're unsure what to imagine, you can look back and review the twelve areas of life listed earlier in this conversation, then pick one area of life where you genuinely desire change.

Take one or two minutes to imagine yourself fully completing that change. Take the time to recognize what kind of emotional response you feel. Feeling it is key.

Now, what change did you just imagine? Describe it in as few or as many words as you wish.

EARN 1 POINT

9. On a scale of 1 to 10, with "1" meaning you couldn't feel any worse and "10" meaning you couldn't feel any better, how good do you feel about your last answer ("question number 8")?

If your answer is a score of 8 or above, write down your score in your diary and then, move on to the next question (question number 10).

However, if your answer is a 7 or below, then how can you change your answer in a way that brings you to a feeling of 8 or above?

Let's move on to the next question (question number 10), only after you have identified a change that genuinely gives you a score of 8 or above.

EARN 1 POINT

10. What will it cost you if you do not take action and make that change?

Consider "cost" in terms of time, money, energy, relationships, reputation, material things, opportunities lost, or something else.

EARN 1 POINT

11. After all this thinking and processing, it's now time to give this change a title or a name. Give it a few words and make it fun if you want.

Ok, so what *short name or title* would you like to give it?

EARN 1 POINT

12. Take a look at a calendar. If you were to actually make this change happen, what is the most earliest date you can imagine completing this change? What month, day, and/or year?

EARN 1 POINT

13. Take a look at a calendar again. When would be the very latest possible date you can imagine completing this change? What month, day, and/or year?

EARN 1 POINT

14. What month, day, and year falls somewhere comfortably between the earliest possible date and the latest possible date?

EARN 1 POINT

(At this point, I'll refer to this change as a "long-term goal," but you can call it the name that you gave it in question number 11 above.)

15. When it comes to your long-term goal, what is one step toward this goal that you can see yourself easily completing within seven days from today?

If you don't know what your first step might be, then what research or investigation could you do in order to find out your first step?

After you write your response, continue to the next question.

EARN 1 POINT

16. You have now written down your next step. This is your first "short-term" goal on your way to your long-term goal.

If you wanted to make this next step even smaller so that you can *be sure to complete it* within the next seven days, what would that smaller step be?

If it seems achievable as is, then just write in your diary that it is achievable as is.

EARN 1 POINT

17. If any negative thoughts are strongly hindering your planning or thinking right now, what are the major ones and how can you challenge them?

Naming negativity has a way of stripping some of its power. For negative thoughts that feel like big obstacles, list the most significant ones. Then, for each one, oppose it with a challenge. For example:

"I don't think I can do it." - Challenge it by writing something like, "I have done things before that I thought I could not do."

"I am not good enough." - Challenge it by writing something like, "It's worth trying and proving that thought wrong."

"I might fail," - Challenge it with something like, "If I don't try at all, that's true failure."

"I don't know how," - Challenge it with something like, "I can learn one small step at a time."

Choose your own words and write them down.

EARN 1 POINT

18. Let's pause for a second to check in on how you feel about these questions you've been answering. How do you feel about the direction you're headed in this exercise right now?

If you feel good, then write a little smiley for this answer and then continue on to the next question.

However, if you feel that you need to go back to an earlier question and change your answer, please do. If you do change an earlier answer, then look at all questions that follow and revise your answers to match your new direction.

When you're ready, let's move on to the next question.

EARN 1 POINT

19. By now, you've written down your next step (or short-term goal) toward your long-term goal, and you have broken it down into something small enough to complete within one week from today.

What's going to be the tangible, material, measurable, or physical evidence that you completed this step? In other words, how will you know that you completed it?

EARN 1 POINT

20. On a scale of 1 to 10, with 10 meaning that you couldn't be any more committed and 1 meaning you couldn't be any less committed, how committed are you to completing that next step?

EARN 1 POINT

21. If you scored a 7 or below in that question (question number 20), how can you change your next step so that it is a score of 8 or above for you?

If you scored an 8 or above already, put a little smiley face in your diary and continue to the next question.

Wait to proceed to the next question until you have a next step that gives you a score of 8 or above.

EARN 1 POINT

22. Over the next week, on what day (or days) will you plan to complete your next step?

EARN 1 POINT

23. How will you remind yourself to complete this? For example, a calendar reminder, an alarm, a paper posted somewhere visible, etc.

EARN 1 POINT

24. How believable is it for you that you can do this?

EARN 1 POINT

25. What can get in the way of you completing this on the day or days that you planned? For each obstacle, explain how you can best prepare for it ahead of time.

List the obstacle and then next to it, write how you can best prepare for it.

EARN 1 POINT

26. What kind of support and accountability, if any, can you use to help ensure that you complete this next step?

EARN 1 POINT

27. After you have completed the action that you set out to do this week, what date do you plan to sit down again for our next "conversation"? Write down your answer.

Remember that momentum gives you strength to complete your long-term goal, and momentum is lost the longer you wait. So, to keep momentum, return here to continue your work in this book as closely as possible to seven days from today.

MAXIMUM POINTS EARNED FOR THIS CHAPTER

You earn 1 point for completing each of the 27 questions above for a maximum of 27 points.

Count the number of points you completed and write down the total number on your Scoreboard, as described in Exercise Chapter 1.

CHAPTER 7, YOUR SECOND COACHING CONVERSATION

Let's check in to review what you've accomplished so far in your personal coaching journey.

- You identified your motivators.
- You have taken a deep inventory of what you want or need the most right now.
- You defined a long-term goal.
- You designed the next small step (short-term goal) that leads you to your long-term goal.

In our last "conversation" in Chapter 6, you discovered a long-term goal, or what I like to call a "destination."

YOUR DESTINATION

A destination is a "long-term" goal, but the amount of time meant by "long-term" depends on your life circumstances. Some people have so many uncertainties about their future that one month for them is "long term," while others can easily plan for a decade or several decades ahead.

However, according to my own experience as a coach, as well as past ICF global coaching studies, coaches and clients tend to work together on 6 to 12-month long-term goals.[6]

But there's a problem with the word "goal."

"Goal" often brings to mind sports imagery of a direct and straight-forward movement of a ball into a net. Reaching life goals, however, aren't as direct as that, especially long-term ones. Rather, when you work on achieving something long-term, there are many windy roads to turn, unexpected detours, and signs to look out for and follow. It's not straight and direct like kicking a ball into a net.

So, the path from right now until you achieve something is far more like a road trip than a sports goal. Because of that, instead of "long-term goal," I like to call it your *destination*.

From this point forward, I'll often refer to your long-term goal as your destination.

You named your destination in our last conversation (Chapter 6 Exercise), and you have started your journey toward reaching it with your first short term goal.

Assuming you have completed or attempted to complete your short term goal from that exercise, in the next exercise, it's time to plan your *next stop* (or next short term goal) on the way to your destination.

YOUR NEXT STOP

Our first conversation is what I call your destination conversation because it's where you identify your long-term goal; it's like picking a destination for a long road trip ahead. Each conversation after that is for planning your next step toward your long-term goal, and so I call it your *next stop* conversation.

When you get in the car and go for a long road trip, you will often pull over or stop so you can rest, eat, refuel, and re-strategize the journey if needed. It's the same with your destination. During the months or weeks that you move toward your long-term goal, each coaching conversation is like a "next stop" along the way to reflect, refuel, and strategize (or sometimes *re*-strategize) your journey.

In personal coaching, you keep creating a new next stop with each conversation, until you finally reach your destination. In each next stop conversation, you generally create a short-term goal to complete either between coaching conversations or within one week, whichever comes first.

The reason there's a time constraint is to keep momentum.

In each conversation as your personal coach, I am like your chauffeur; I drive our conversations with coaching questions, tools, and techniques, until you hit all your short terms goals and finally reach your destination.

It's my job to keep an eye on the clock to ensure we are on time and to help you keep moving.

I follow the "road signs," such as your non-verbal communication, to avoid hazards.

I remain aware of the direction of the conversation to make sure it's accomplishing the plan you set.

WHAT'S THE DIFFERENCE BETWEEN A DESTINATION AND NEXT STOP CONVERSATION?

The difference between those two types of conversations is in the outcome.

Your destination conversation covers the purpose for the coaching relationship and ends with two results - a measurable long-term goal (your destination) and a first measurable short-term goal (your next step or action).

Your next conversation (and every conversation thereafter) is called your "next stop conversation," and each one of those conversations end with one result - to design your next short-term goal that moves you closer toward your destination.

The results of both conversations are to identify measurable actions. We work toward something you can say you have completed.

Until you reach your destination, we continue having next stop conversations. Once you reach your destination, whether it is a new career, a new home, a better relationship, etc., you can start working on a brand-new destination for your life.

WHAT IF MY GOAL IS NOT MEASURABLE BUT IS ONLY EMOTIONAL?

We call goals "measurable" so that you can clearly mark the moment that you achieve it, and then know when to celebrate. When you have an emotional goal, such as "to feel happier" or "to be more confident," it can be a bit more difficult to identify when you've fully achieved them. Since emotions are much harder to measure, when you have a goal that's emotional, I refer to them as meta-goals.

There are procedures and medical equipment that can measure your heart rate, hormone levels, body chemistry levels, and brain activity which could potentially make meta-goals more measurable. But at this point in history, we're only living in the beginning of the 21st century and that kind of equipment is not easily accessible to the general public for the purposes of coaching.

Maybe that'll change in the coming years and we'll each be able to measure our exact emotional states at home with a reliable piece of equipment.

Emotional goals are the goal behind your goal, so they are your "meta-goals."

For example, one of my clients has a meta-goal of peace and clarity in her career. We can't put peace and clarity in a cup or on a scale at this point in history and science; there's no stable physical evidence to indicate she's sustainably or adequately achieved it.

Her measurable goal or destination, however, is to start her own business, which she does believe will bring more peace and clarity in her career - more than her current role. The goal of starting a business does offer physical and digital evidence such as the legal business registration documents, completing a marketing campaign, and receipts from sales. Those are things we can observe or measure.

So, when I work with a client on a goal, the emotional goal (or meta-goal) is important to know, but a measurable goal is what we use to design action and track progress.

WHAT IF I CHANGE MY MIND?

If, at some point along the journey, you discover the destination that you've been working toward is not right for you, then it's my duty as your personal coach to return to the destination conversation to help you revise your long-term goal until it's right for you.

It's ok to reroute the path you're taking.

Whether you look under a microscope or look out into the universe through a telescope, you will see that the entire world is constantly in flux, moving and changing. Everything worthwhile needs revisiting to keep it current and healthy.

In life, new roads are built, some roads are shut down, and it might be the same with the roads of your life. As you grow and adapt your needs and wants may change which, in turn, changes your destination.

This is your journey. If at any point you feel you need to begin a new direction in life, we can return to the destination conversation to start again with a stronger vision.

Once you find a destination the fits your sense of purpose and meaning, you will not see any other option than to drive your life toward it. When you feel that the goal is more true to you, then you will stay more committed.

ARE THERE OTHER KINDS OF CONVERSATIONS YOU CAN HAVE?

The destination conversation aims to define your long-term goal, and all conversations after that are called "next stop conversations" until you reach your long-term goal. In each next stop conversation, we set up your next short-term goal that moves you closer to your long-term one.

When you reach your destination, we return to back to having a new destination conversation to find your next long-term goal.

That's it, except for one thing.

At some point, it's possible that I jump on a call with you for a coaching conversation only to find that you're going through an unexpected, urgent, or simply a highly emotional situation that completely distracts you from your long-term goal. So, before we can start working directly on your destination, we have to clear the roadway.

In that kind of situation, we would have what I call a "Detour Conversation."

DETOUR CONVERSATION

During a "next stop" conversation, I might discover that you are experiencing something that you see as unavoidable and that steers you away from direct progress toward your destination. If that happens, then we might spend that conversation working on a separate short-term goal.

This separate short-term goal may not appear to directly move you toward your long-term goal. However, it is necessary for you to move forward so that you can get back "on the road" to your destination.

Detours can often appear to move you in a different direction than intended - even in an opposite direction for a time, but they are necessary to follow for your health and sanity; otherwise, you may not reach your long-term goal at all!

However, if detours extend to two or three conversations, then it's time to revisit whether the destination needs revising to a new goal that may be more relevant to your current needs and life situation. And if so, that's simply a matter of returning to the Destination Conversation.

EXERCISE (CHAPTER 7)

In your diary, write today's date and "Chapter 7" on top of the page.

Welcome to our second coaching conversation, which I call our "next stop conversation." Our last conversation in Chapter 6 concluded with a long term goal and your next step of action.

Now in Chapter 7, you will need around one hour of private and uninterrupted time, the same I hope you were able to do in the last exercise.

If you attempted your action but didn't complete it, we'll address that today.

This Chapter 7 exercise is now another "coaching conversation," but it is designed to help you identify your next step or *next stop* on the way to your long-term goal. There are 28 questions intended to help you step by step.

Ready? Take your time to write down each question with your most honest and heart-felt answers.

EARN 1 POINT

1. Before we get started, how much time have you set aside right now to answer the questions in this exercise?

EARN 1 POINT

2. How safe and distraction-free is your environment right now? If you don't feel good about your answer, what can you do right now to make it better for you?

EARN 1 POINT

3. In the last exercise, you planned a next step toward your destination. What would you like to say about what you've done or haven't done regarding that step?

EARN 1 POINT

4. What, if anything, did you observe or learn about *yourself* regarding that next step? It may be anything - very big or very small.

EARN 1 POINT

5. What are some things that you'd like to think about right now that would help move you closer to your destination in a positive way?

EARN 1 POINT

6. On a scale of 1 to 10, with 10 meaning it couldn't be any better and 1 meaning it couldn't be any worse, how good do you feel right now about your destination (long-term goal)?

EARN 1 POINT

7. If you gave a score of 8 or above, draw a smiley face in your diary for this question and then continue to the next question below.

If you gave a score of 7 or below, what could do or change to bring that score back up to an 8 or above?

For example, one thing you could do is revisit the destination conversation to more clearly define or possibly even *re*define your destination. If that sounds right for you, then please stop here, do not proceed to the next question, and instead return to the last chapter's exercise and redo the destination conversation from beginning to end on a new page of your diary.

After you follow that process, I'll see you back here when you have a better and more empowering destination.

EARN 1 POINT

8. Now that we know you're feeling good about your destination, it's time to move closer toward it.

What do you believe would be the most meaningful short-term goal (next stop) that you believe you can complete *within the next seven days*?

Ensure it's sized to fit into your schedule within the next seven days.

EARN 1 POINT

9. In the last question, you described a next stop or next step of action. If you could make your next stop align more closely with your motivators, how would you change it?

EARN 1 POINT

10. Imagine that you already completed your next stop and that you did everything in your control that you could do to make it happen.

Now, think about what's "in your control" to make it happen. What is a list of things (big or small) that are in your own control about this next stop?

EARN 1 POINT

11. By now, you have described a meaningful and important next stop (short-term goal) that aligns with your motivators.

If you completed your next stop, in what way(s) might it move you closer toward your destination?

EARN 1 POINT

12. What will it cost you if you do *not* complete your next stop? The cost can be in terms of time, money, energy, relationships, reputation, material things, or something else.

EARN 1 POINT

13. If your next stop had a title, like the name of a road or a place, what would the name be?
In other words, what is a short name or title you can give your next stop?

EARN 1 POINT

14. On a scale of 1 to 10, how important is it to you that you complete your next stop? A score of 10 means that it couldn't be any more important, and 1 means that it couldn't be any less important.
If your score is an 8 or above, give yourself a smiley face for this question and continue to the next question.
Did you score a 7 or below? If you did, what could you change about your next stop that would make it an 8 or above in its level of importance to you? Make adjustments to your next stop until you can give a score of 8 or above.

EARN 1 POINT

15. You're reading this question because you now have a next stop with a score of 8 or above.
In what, if any, way can you make this step even smaller so that you feel 100% confident you can achieve it within seven days from today?

EARN 1 POINT

16. What's the least amount of minutes or hours it could take for you to complete it, and what's the most amount of minutes or hours that it could take?

EARN 1 POINT

17. If a negative thought is hindering your planning or thinking right now, what is that thought and what, if anything, might be false about it?
List any negative or hindering thoughts and imagine in what very small or big way they may potentially be proven wrong.

EARN 1 POINT

18. Let's pause for just a second to check in to see how you feel at this moment. How do you feel about the direction you're headed in this exercise right now?

If you feel good, please continue with the exercise.

If you feel that you need to go back to an earlier question and change your answer, please do. Then, go through the questions you already answered and write down new answers based on your new direction.

Then, when you're ready, let's move on to the next question.

EARN 1 POINT

19. What's going to be the tangible, material, or measurable evidence that you completed the step you identified in question number 16? In other words, what will be the physical or digital sign that you completed it?

EARN 1 POINT

20. On a scale of 1 to 10, with 10 meaning you couldn't be any more committed and 1 meaning you couldn't be any less committed, how committed are you to taking that small step?

If you scored an 8 or above, give yourself another smiley face and let's continue to the next question.

If you scored a 7 or below, what can you adjust about your next step so that it gives you a score of an 8 or above?

If you adjusted your next stop after reading this question, then please return to question number 13 above to re-name it if necessary, and then re-answer all questions that followed (14 to 20) so that your answers match your new short term goal.

EARN 1 POINT

21. On what day (or days) will you complete this step?

For example, it might be all done in one hour on Sunday or you might split it into smaller 20 minute time slots spread across three different weekdays.

EARN 1 POINT

22. In what way will you remind yourself to complete this? For example, a calendar reminder, an alarm, a paper posted somewhere visible, etc.

EARN 1 POINT

23. How believable is it to you that you can do this?

If you doubt that you can do it, what will you change so that you believe that you can?

EARN 1 POINT

24. What can get in the way of you completing this on the day (or days) that you planned? List each obstacle and explain how you can best prepare for each one ahead of time.

EARN 1 POINT

25. You've designed your next stop; however, if there are any other additional tasks, to-do's, or actions on your mind that will bring you closer to your destination, list them now so that you can use refer back to them when you plan another next stop. If you don't want to, just draw a smiley and move on to the next question.

EARN 1 POINT

26. What kind of support and accountability, if any, can you plan for that will possibly help ensure you complete this action?

EARN 1 POINT

27. Let's look at a date and time for our next conversation. This date would be after you complete your next step. It will require another dedicated time of sitting in a private place with this exercise for anywhere from 30 minutes to an hour. What date works best and what time slot works best for you on that date?

Remember that, to stay motivated and keep you moving forward, it's essential to take your next step of action and return to these exercises *within one week*.

EARN 1 POINT

28. Celebrating even your small wins (or if you didn't "win," then celebrating things you learned) will create momentum.

In what way, if any, would you like to celebrate your effort so far? For example, you may want to grab your favorite coffee, go on a five-minute reflective walk, do something artistic or creative, turn on a favorite song to feel good, grab food that you love, tell someone, or buy something special.

MAXIMUM POINTS EARNED FOR THIS CHAPTER

You earn 1 point for answering each of the questions above for a maximum of 28 points.

Count the number of points you earned in this chapter exercise and write down the total on your Scoreboard, as described in Exercise Chapter 1.

Optionally, after you answer all of these questions and after you complete the next step that you planned, you can return again and again to this same list of 28 questions in order to come up with your *next* "next stop."

Then, repeat the cycle of designing action (through these questions) and then taking action, until you reach your destination.

You can even write your answers into your diary each time you do it, but note that you only earn 28 points on your Scoreboard for the first time you complete this chapter exercise.

CHAPTER 8, THE SEVEN GEARS

Let's review how far you've come, through our coaching relationship.

- You identified your motivators.
- You have taken a deep inventory of what you want or need the most right now.
- You defined a long-term goal.
- You designed your "next stop" (next small step, short-term goal) that leads you to your long-term goal.
- And you may have even completed the action you designed in the last "next stop conversation."

HOW TO REACH YOUR DESTINATION

I designed the questions in the previous chapter exercise (Chapter 7) so that you can keep repeating that list of questions until you reach your destination. In other words, after you complete your "next stop," return to the list of questions in Chapter 7 to come up with your next step of action, and repeat until you reach your destination.

Once you reach your destination, you can return to the questions in Chapter 6 to identify a *new* destination (long-term goal).

Simply set time aside once a week (or more often if you want) to do that, and use a fresh page in your diary each time.

While you work on reaching your destination, continue reading this book and completing the rest of its exercises to find out what's going on behind the scenes of a coaching conversation. Doing both will allow you to cover both the theory and the practice of *The Science of Personal Coaching*.

WRITTEN CONVERSATIONS VS. LIVE CONVERSATIONS

While the previous exercises gave you a small taste of what a coaching conversation is like and in what order questions generally happen, a written version of a coaching conversation is, of course, *not* fluid like a live one.

For example, in a live conversation, I would customize the questions to your specific emotional or mental state as I observe it changing, taking note of your nonverbal cues or hearing your tone of voice.

Your words, tones, and various levels of reaction at each stage of our conversation help me determine which tools and techniques to use to help you get clarity and take action. Being able to gauge your reaction helps me understand which direction to go and, most importantly, how fast to move.

When speaking live, I can shift gears at any moment based on my observations. When it's a pre-written conversation, I have assumed specific places or likely points where you can optionally shift down or up a gear.

That "shifting" I do during our conversation is what I call "The Seven Gears of Every Coaching Conversation," which I also introduced in an article I published on The International Coach Federation's website.[7]

In this and the next several chapters, I'll go deeper into this theory and take you behind the scenes of what happens in each stage of the process.

THE SEVEN GEARS OF EVERY COACHING CONVERSATION

You know the stick or "gear shift" that you move in a manual car? Well, on that stick, you typically see five numbered gears (1-5) plus two letter gears ("R" for reverse and "N" for neutral), for a total of seven. It's the same with coaching. There are seven gears I'll move through as your coach.

If you've ever driven a stick shift car, you'll know you start in first, shift up to second, then third, fourth, and up to fifth gear. When it's a simple and direct journey, gears move sequentially.

Roads aren't typically simple or direct, however. So, in a car, you also shift up, then down, then back up again. Sometimes, when you are in fifth gear, you will press the break to slow down as you exit a highway, and then switch to second gear to drive the exit ramp.

It's the same in coaching conversations. It's not always simple and direct from start to finish. Rather, as your coach, I may need to downshift from a high gear to a low and then, return to a higher gear again.

Just like the gears of a manual car's stick shift:

- First gear is the slowest part of the conversation and is only concerned with getting the conversation on and started.
- Second, third, and fourth gears are when I move you forward toward your destination with clarity about what you want. We carefully follow signs to find and name your goal.
- Fifth gear is the highest and fastest gear, like an expressway or highway to your goal; it's when I help you create action.
- Reverse gear gets you out of mentally "stuck" place.
- Neutral gear helps you move more smoothly through all other gears.

Learning to drive a manual car or stick shift for the first time can feel incredibly nerve-wracking because there are so many moving parts to coordinate all at once. You may think you'll never get the hang of it, until one day when you do.

It just takes a lot of practice. Moving smoothly through the seven gears of coaching will require lots of practice, too.

WHAT HAPPENS IN EACH GEAR?

After this chapter, I give each gear its own chapter, and I share with you what is meant to take place in each gear.

As introduced at the beginning of this book, coaching conversations have two parts - getting clarity, and then designing motivated action. That's it. Every time.

That means that, as your coach, in every conversation I will use several coaching skills, tools, and techniques to help you get clear on what you want, and then I'll help you create an inspiring next step of action to get it.

The process of getting clarity and then designing action is like the process of shifting the gears of a car to get somewhere; there are seven movements that I take you through.

However, when it comes to the seven gears, something important to note here is that I'm sharing the theory with you in this book, bringing you "behind the scenes," but I don't use most of these words in the conversation itself. In other words, in a live coaching conversation, you won't hear me talk about or even mention the word "gear" (or "gears").

Gear is not a word that I say to you at any point when I'm coaching you. Rather, the idea of the seven gears is a mental process to follow so that I know I'm doing my job and giving you, my client, all the tools, skills, and techniques you need to make magic happen.

And here they are.

First Gear. Seek agreement.

It's like getting the car started and ready for the drive.

I seek your agreement on the logistics for the conversation, or the generally *un*emotional basics like the conversation time frame, whether you're comfortable and ready for the conversation, find a more stable internet connection if needed, or discuss what I offer and what you expect from coaching.

Second Gear. Enter heart space.

This gear is the beginning of acceleration.

It's when I start looking into what really matters to you today and right now, a topic that I call "heart space."

I start to find out how you feel and what's on your mind at the moment. Finding this out can often require a braindump of everything that's top of your mind. In this gear, you might not yet know exactly what you want to get out of today's coaching conversation.

Third Gear. Find the fire.

This gear is like reaching a steady speed, then driving through windy roads in search of the ramp that takes you to the highway.

In this gear, I seek out a metaphorical fire burning somewhere in you. This fire represents what you want most strongly right now, based on all the things you talked about in first and second gear.

Sometimes, you'll fly past second gear and immediately into third, telling me right away what you would like to get from the coaching conversation. Other times, you may be cruising in second gear for a while until I find your fire.

In other words, this gear is the one in which I discover what goal or next step lights you up the most, and I refer to this gear as "fire" since it's the spark that we're after.

Fourth Gear. Write words.

This gear is like finding the ramp that takes you onto the highway and then gaining enough speed to merge with the fast-moving traffic.

In fourth gear, I find the "write" words. That's an intentional pun to "find the *right* words."

At this point, I write down the most accurate or right words that you have given me to describe your next step toward your goal. In other words, you give your *next stop* a name.

In fourth gear, it's important for me to use your exact name and language for your vision, because then you are more likely to be committed to it and better understand what it entails.

Fifth Gear. Design action.

This gear is like driving highest speed down the highway.

At this point in the conversation, you are emotionally full speed toward your destination. You know what you want, and you feel great about it. Now, it's simply a matter of getting clear on what the very first stop looks like and how to best get it on your calendar.

While the previous gears focus on getting clarity, this gear is the only one in which we focus on action.

Neutral Gear. Check in.

This gear allows us to pause our conversation to make sure we are headed in the direction you intended.

I check in with you to see if you'd like to keep going the same "speed" or if we need to switch into another gear. In other words, it's a chance to check in to see if you're happy with the conversation.

I can shift us into neutral during any gear, but, ideally, it happens anytime between third and fifth gear, and this check-in happens at least once every conversation.

One of the simplest and clearest way for me to check in is to ask, "How do you feel about the direction of the conversation so far?"

Reverse Gear. Overcome.

This is the gear where I pull out coaching tools to help you back out of thought processes where you lose clarity or feel stuck. In short, this is about overcoming obstacles.

Sometimes a path of conversation, thought, or topic can feel like accidentally driving into a parking space that's littered with broken glass or nails. If we metaphorically "drive into that spot," it will puncture your tire and prevent you from moving forward. So, to address those moments, I shift into reverse gear.

Reverse gear can happen at any point in the conversation, whenever we back out of perspectives or directions of conversation that threaten your sense of motivation or that halt forward-movement toward your destination. *The Science of Personal Coaching* will show you several techniques used in this gear to get you unstuck.

GEAR CHAPTER FORMAT

Each gear's chapter has the same format, designed to help you understand the process of a coaching conversation, and each one is broken down into the following headings:
- DEFINITION
- CHECKLIST
- TECHNIQUES AND TOOLS
- COACHING QUESTIONS
- ICF CORE COMPETENCIES

The "Definition" section will give you an overview of the gear.

The "Checklist" section contains the list of actions that a coach properly takes within that gear, not necessarily in the order listed. The checklists themselves are never discussed or addressed directly with clients; rather, they are a coach's professional process that a great coach will use behind the scenes during the conversation. It's helpful for coaches to print them out and silently glance at them during coaching conversations to ensure they're on track with their clients.

"Techniques and Tools" shares some of the key coaching skills that help the coach accomplish the purpose of that specific gear.

"Coaching Questions" are examples of questions that help me, as your coach, accomplish the purposes (or checklist items) of the specific gear. There are hundreds more questions than those you will see listed in this section, but what you read will offer a good example of the kinds of questions you can expect.

The "ICF Core Competencies" is a very brief note about how the gear might relate to ICF's published standards. It's a short and sweet reminder, for those who want to know.

Each gear is also followed by an exercise that allows you to think more deeply about what you read, apply it to your life, challenge you to take action, and collect points along the way.

Ready to get on the road?

EXERCISE (CHAPTER 8)

In your diary, write today's date and "Chapter 8" on top of the page.

This exercise is a matching game.

Because I introduced you to each of the seven gears in this chapter, let's see if you can now match each of the following 27 coaching conversation questions to one of the seven gears.

Write down a numbered list from 1 to 27 in your diary, and for each question below, pick one gear that you believe the question most closely matches. Use the section in this chapter titled, "What happens in each gear?"

EARN 1 POINT

1. To which of the seven gears does this question belong?

Before we get started, how much time do you have to spend today on this exercise?

EARN 1 POINT

2. To which of the seven gears does this question belong?

How safe and distraction-free is your environment right now? If you don't feel good about your answer, what can you do right now to make it better for you?

EARN 1 POINT

3. To which of the seven gears does this question belong?

In the last exercise, you planned a next step toward your destination. What would you like to say about what you've done or haven't done regarding this step?

EARN 1 POINT

4. To which of the seven gears does this question belong?

What did you learn about yourself regarding that next step? It may be anything - very big or very small.

EARN 1 POINT

5. To which of the seven gears does this question belong?

What are some things that you'd like to think about right now that would move you closer to your destination?

EARN 1 POINT

6. To which of the seven gears does this question belong?

On a scale of 1 to 10, with 10 meaning it couldn't be any better and 1 meaning it couldn't be any worse, how good do you feel right now about your destination (long-term goal) right now?

EARN 1 POINT

7. To which of the seven gears does this question belong?

If you gave a score of 8 or above, write a smiley face in your diary for this question (question number 7) and continue to the next question.

If you gave a score of 7 or below, what could do or change to bring that back up to an 8 or above?

One thing you could do is revisit the destination conversation to more clearly define or possibly even redefine your destination. If that sounds right for you, then please stop here, do not proceed to the next question, and instead return to the last chapter's exercise and redo the destination conversation from beginning to end on a new page of your diary.

EARN 1 POINT

8. To which of the seven gears does this question belong?

It's time to move closer toward your destination. What do you believe would be the most meaningful short-term goal (next stop) that you believe you can complete within the next seven days?

EARN 1 POINT

9. To which of the seven gears does this question belong?

If you could make your next stop align more closely with your motivators, how would you change it?

EARN 1 POINT

10. To which of the seven gears does this question belong?

By now, you have described a meaningful and important next stop (short-term goal) that aligns with your motivators. If you can be even more specific, how would you describe your next stop? Write out a couple of ways that it can actually happen. Be creative.

EARN 1 POINT

11. To which of the seven gears does this question belong?

What will it cost you if you do not complete your next stop? The cost can be in terms of time, money, energy, relationships, reputation, material things, or something else.

EARN 1 POINT

12. To which of the seven gears does this question belong?

Your next stop is something that you're completing within the next seven days. In a perfect world, by which particular day would you complete the next stop?

EARN 1 POINT

13. To which of the seven gears does this question belong?

Over the next seven days, when would be the latest possible day that you can imagine completing it by?

EARN 1 POINT

14. To which of the seven gears does this question belong?

On a scale of 1 to 10, how important is it to you that you complete your next stop? A score of 10 means that it couldn't be any more important, and 1 means that it couldn't be any less important.

EARN 1 POINT

15. To which of the seven gears does this question belong?

If your score is an 8 or above, give yourself a smiley face for this question and continue to the next question.

Did you score a 7 or below? If you did, what could you change about your next stop that would make it an 8 or above in its level of importance to you?

EARN 1 POINT

16. To which of the seven gears does this question belong?

Okay, you are reading this question because you now have a next stop with a score of 8 or above.

In what, if any, way can you make this step even smaller so that you feel 100% confident you can achieve it within seven days from today?

EARN 1 POINT

17. To which of the seven gears does this question belong?

If a negative thought is hindering your planning or thinking right now, what is that thought and how true is it? List each negative thought and then next to each one, write the percentage of how true and false it might be. For example, you may write something like, "My boss won't let me do it. Maybe 40% true, 60% false."

EARN 1 POINT

18. To which of the seven gears does this question belong?

Let's pause for just a second to check in to see how you feel at this moment. How do you feel about the direction you're headed in this exercise right now?

If you feel good, please continue with the exercise.

If you feel that you need to go back to an earlier question and change your answer, please do. Then, go through the questions you already answered and write down new answers based on your new direction.

Then, when you're ready, let's move on to the next question.

EARN 1 POINT

19. To which of the seven gears does this question belong?

What's going to be the tangible, material, measurable, or evidence that you completed the step you identified in question number 16? In other words, what will be the physical sign that you completed it?

EARN 1 POINT

20. To which of the seven gears does this question belong?

On a scale of 1 to 10, with 10 meaning you couldn't be any more committed and 1 meaning you couldn't be any less committed, how committed are you to taking that small step?

EARN 1 POINT

21. To which of the seven gears does this question belong?

If you scored an 8 or above, give yourself another smiley face and let's continue to the next question.

If you scored a 7 or below, change your next step until it gives you a score of an 8 or above.

EARN 1 POINT

22. To which of the seven gears does this question belong?
On what day or days will you complete this step?

EARN 1 POINT

23. To which of the seven gears does this question belong?

In what way will you remind yourself to complete this? For example, a calendar reminder, an alarm, a paper posted somewhere visible, etc.

EARN 1 POINT

24. To which of the seven gears does this question belong?
How believable is it to you that you can do this?

EARN 1 POINT

25. To which of the seven gears does this question belong?
What can get in the way of you completing this on the day or days that you planned? List each obstacle and explain how you can best prepare for each one ahead of time.

EARN 1 POINT

26. To which of the seven gears does this question belong?
What kind of support and accountability, if any, can you plan to use to help ensure you complete this action?

EARN 1 POINT

27. To which of the seven gears does this question belong?
In what way can you celebrate your effort this past week? For example, you may want to grab your favorite coffee, go on a five-minute reflective walk, do something artistic or creative, turn on a favorite song, grab food that you love, tell someone, or buy something special.

MAXIMUM POINTS EARNED FOR THIS CHAPTER

You earn 1 point for answering each of the questions above for a maximum of 27 points.

Count the number of points you completed and write down the total number on your Scoreboard, as described in Exercise Chapter 1.

CHAPTER 9, FIRST GEAR - SEEK AGREEMENT

DEFINITION

We begin in first gear. It's when I seek out an agreement on the generally unemotional basics, such as the logistics for the conversation and general expectations about coaching.

By "logistics," I mean confirming our intended duration of the conversation, the stability of the technical connection (e.g., phone call, video conference, in-person meeting), any necessary materials or pen/paper/tablet for the conversation, new contact information or updates, and any other preparation.

As your coach, it's important that I not *assume* your agreement to anything. So, in this gear, we also come to an understanding of what's going to take place.

CHECKLIST

If I've never spoken with you before as your coach, then my very first coaching conversation with you (our "destination conversation") takes a bit longer than all other conversations.

The first time we speak, we have more logistics and agreement items to cover about our coaching relationship. However, after you have reached your destination and want to work on a new long-term goal, we return to the "destination conversation" but I don't have to repeat the items we already agreed to the first time around.

Now, without further ado, below you'll see the first gear checklist that I follow for destination conversations where we design a long-term goal, and below that, you'll see the first gear checklist for every conversation afterward, otherwise called "next stop conversations."

First Gear Checklist (Destination Conversations)

- ☑ Confirm today's time frame and any other logistics for the conversation
- ☑ Affirm a safe space
- ☑ Allow silent pauses for processing

When speaking with a client for the first time:

- ☑ Describe client-centricity
- ☑ Cover cancellations, lateness, and rescheduling
- ☑ Provide coaching definition (clarity and action)
- ☑ Cover confidentiality
- ☑ Discuss permission
- ☑ Permission to take notes
- ☑ Effectiveness depends on regularly scheduled conversations
- ☑ Review communication technology options for our conversations
- ☑ Five Assumptions (knowledge, honesty, resources, false assumptions, emotional ends)
- ☑ Your decisions are 100% up to you, not me
- ☑ Coach's availability and responsiveness

✅ Answer any of client's questions about coaching

First Gear Checklist (Next Stop Conversations)

✅ Confirm today's time frame and any other logistics for the conversation
✅ Affirm a safe space
✅ Allow silent pauses for processing

TECHNIQUES AND TOOLS

A "Techniques and Tools" section, like this one, will appear in each of the following gear chapters. It's like a little toolbox specifically for that gear. Pick and choose; use what you need.

Most tools and techniques in these sections will not appear on the checklists. That's because they are only pulled out of the "toolbox" if or when they are needed. Sometimes I may use only one of them in a gear, and other times I'll use a few.

However, one of the tools and techniques that you will see on the first gear checklist is "Affirming a Safe Space," and that's because it sets a foundation for you, as the client, to speak freely for all the other gears.

If I wait until fourth gear to "affirm a safe space," then I may discover that you were uncomfortable, distracted, or nervous throughout all of the previous gears, and your answers were half-hearted or not true for you. The conversation, in that case, wasn't effective, and we would have to start over. So, affirming a safe space sets the stage.

Here below are other items in the first gear toolbox.

1. Asking Permission

In a written coaching contract or terms and conditions, you give me your permission to keep you accountable to your goals. However, a formal contract may not directly cover every form of permission that's required during a conversation such as permission to interrupt, take notes, or make an observation.

An important ethic of professional coaching is to make no assumptions about having your permission. So, during our live conversation, I might ask you permission for many things in order to make you feel comfortable, to instill trust, and to put the power of every decision into your own hands.

I may ask permission at any point in the conversation, but first gear is the standard place where key permission-based questions show up, such as:

- "To keep you accountable to your goal, are you comfortable if I interrupt when I notice us going off track?"
- "Are you ok if I take notes at different points in the conversation? This helps me remember what's important to you."
- "Would you like me to use text messages to remind you of your next stop or would you prefer a different communication tool?"
- More permission-based questions show up in other gears, including:
- "Would you like hear an observation about that?"
- "What are your thoughts on brainstorming some ideas?"

- After fifth gear before we end the conversation, I might also ask your permission about how you prefer to be supported in your goals, such as:
- "After this conversation, would you like me to summarise your next stop and email it to you?"
- "Would you like me to email you a list of observations from today's conversation, send it on WhatsApp, or something else?"

2. Coaching Chemistry

Princeton researchers showed that it took only 100 milliseconds to like or dislike a person.[8] Milliseconds! And that first feeling doesn't go away. It sticks.[9]

An automatic sense of respect or inspiration is key to a coaching relationship. In other words, "coaching chemistry" is a must.

If you're paying for my services out of your own pocket, then you're not going to keep paying me if you feel uncomfortable, disinterested, repulsed by, or bored by my personality. Our conversations won't flow naturally or easily, and you may not get anything useful out of the conversation.

Likewise, if you feel excited by who I am naturally, then your success as my client has great potential to skyrocket. That is what I call coaching chemistry. It's a natural and mutual sense of high regard between the both of us, and it's a tool to determine whether I'm the right fit for you and whether you're the right fit for me.

When a coach and client come together, it can be like the whip cream on a sundae, or it can be like whip cream on dry meatloaf. It's simply who the coach is and who the client is at the time they enter the coaching relationship.

It's a matter of either having an instant connection or the opposite - relational dissonance, and it's a real phenomenon studied within psychology and related fields.[10]

Here is a list of things that for me, subconscious or conscious, can potentially determine coaching chemistry to varying degrees:

- Listening skills
- Career or education background
- Shared special interests
- Traits such as confidence, intelligence, or zest for life
- Vocal tones, pitch, or patterns
- Looks or acts in a way that is familiar to people I know or admire
- Facial expressions
- Fashion or personal style
- Achievements in life

3. Affirming a Safe Space

As your coach, I like to say at the beginning of the conversation something like, "I want to remind you at the beginning of every conversation that this is a safe space for you to be yourself and not hold back what you truly think or want."

It can be said in many ways, but it's a "safe space affirmation."

When a coach says something ceremonial like this in every conversation, it reminds you that you've entered a very different kind of conversation. A verbal reminder like this over the phone can also have a similar effect to you walking into my office, shutting the office door for privacy, and falling onto the comfy pillows of my office sofa.

On a phone call or video chat, you don't have a view of the whole room where I'm sitting which means you might not feel assured of your privacy and confidentiality; so, verbally affirming it for you let's you know that it's important to me and that it's in place.

COACHING QUESTIONS

The following are only some examples of the kinds of questions I might ask in order to tick all the boxes required in first gear.

There are two lists of questions below - one for all clients, and then a list of additional questions for brand new clients.

The conversation with brand new clients involves important introductory information about coaching that I will not bring up again in a future conversation. The questions that I choose to ask new clients also depends on how much the client already knows or already agreed to.

First Gear Questions

- You have scheduled __ minutes with me today. Is that still a good time frame?
- Do you feel that you're in a safe place for talking now?
- Are you ready to get started?
- How ready do you feel for a coaching conversation?
- Can you speak freely?
- Do you have enough privacy right now for our phone call?
- Do you need to take care of any possible distractions before we get started?
- Are you sitting somewhere comfortable?

Additional Questions for a Brand-New Client

- What do you know about coaching?
- What do you hope to get out of coaching?
- What are your expectations for a coaching relationship like this?
- What questions can I answer for you about coaching before we get started?
- What do you want to achieve from coaching?
- Why are you seeking coaching at this time in your life?
- What does being coached mean to you?
- Much of the success of our conversations depends on your degree of feeling safe and comfortable and our degree of personality chemistry. When either of us doesn't feel the chemistry is right or if you simply don't feel comfortable, either of us is free to stop these conversations. Is that okay with you?
- Our conversations will be safe, confidential, and nonjudgmental, which means that I will not judge anything as "right" or "wrong." If there is ever a clear sign of danger to yourself or others, that would be the only exception. How do you feel about that?
- How will you evaluate the success of this coaching service?
- What kind of coach would you like me to be for you?
- What is the most exciting part of being coached for you?
- What is the scariest part of being coached for you?

- What could interrupt our professional relationship?
- What topic would make your coaching experience most worthwhile?
- What goal would make your coaching experience most worthwhile?
- How do you feel about me taking notes during our conversations?
- What, if any, questions do you have about my availability and/or the communications tools we use?

ICF CORE COMPETENCIES

Note:

For each of the next several chapters, I'll include this section ("ICF Core Competencies") for those who are, or who are interested in becoming, an ICF-credentialed coach. These sections only briefly touch on how each gear demonstrates one or several competencies, but they are short and sweet, meant only as a quick reference.

The ICF standards and their "competencies" in this book are current as of the year 2018 and may have been revised since the publication of this book.[11] Where you see quoted phrases in this section, note that this is language I've seen used by ICF.

In first gear, these four (out of a total of eleven) competencies are demonstrated:

- Meeting Ethical Guidelines and Professional Standards,
- Establishing the Coaching Contract,
- Direct Communication, and
- Establishing Trust and Intimacy.

Meeting Ethical Guidelines and Professional Standards

ICF has a rich resource of ethical and professional standards for coaches, all of which a coach can use or reference in their coaching contract as well as share in coaching conversations with new clients.

Establishing the Coaching Contract

When I discuss or present what we agree to in a coaching relationship, I'm safeguarding my client's interests as well as my own. As the ICF says it, I'm discussing the "specific parameters of the coaching relationship."

Direct Communication

From the very beginning of our first conversation, I speak to you, as my client, in an honest way that intends to make you feel respected. I'll also ensure that my language is as "non-sexist, non-racist, non-technical," and free of as much jargon as possible.

Establishing Trust and Intimacy

When I affirm at the start of each of our conversations that you're in a safe space, I'm using ICF's advice to provide "a safe, supportive environment that produces ongoing mutual respect and trust."

EXERCISE (CHAPTER 9)

In your diary, write today's date and "Chapter 9" on top of the page.

Consider the following questions and answer them in your diary. Safety is key. So, these questions aim to help you remember, feel, and imagine the importance of feeling safe in a conversation and the role that environment plays.

EARN 1 POINT

1. Write a few sentences about a time when you wanted to talk about something with someone, but it was not the right physical environment to do so.

Here's an example: *I wanted to tell a friend on the phone about something that happened at work, but I was sitting in a cafe that was next door to my office, and so I felt wary that co-workers may come in and overhear me.*

EARN 1 POINT

2. Regarding the environment that you described in question number 1, what made you feel uncomfortable about that environment?

Example answer: *The physical environment was too close.*

EARN 1 POINT

3. If that same situation happened again, what would you do differently to ensure a more comfortable environment?

Example answer: *I would text the story instead of saying it out loud and then wait to say it to her until I get home.*

EARN 1 POINT

4. Now, tell me about a time when you were in an environment that helped you feel free and safe to express yourself to someone in a conversation.

EARN 1 POINT

5. Regarding your answer to number 4 above, what specifically about the environment made you feel safe and open to talking?

MAXIMUM POINTS EARNED FOR THIS CHAPTER

You earn 1 point for completing each of the 5 questions above for a maximum of 5 points.

Count the number of points you completed and write down the total number on your Scoreboard, as described in Exercise Chapter 1.

CHAPTER 10, SECOND GEAR - ENTER HEART SPACE

DEFINITION

Second gear is an early stage of the process of getting clarity, and we do this by sorting through all of the things on your mind or more importantly, whatever is "in your heart."

When I shift the conversation into second gear, we move out of the topic of logistics (time, internet or phone connection, etc.), and I focus more closely on your emotional state. Your emotional state is what I call heart space, and I use that phrase because it points to a physical place in your body. Usually, people feel emotions most significantly in either their chest near their heart or somewhere in the abdomen.

So how do I move our focus to heart space? Exploring your heart space often requires a brain dump - or "braindump" which I like to write as one word. A braindump can powerfully help you connect with how you're feeling and address anything that may be distracting you. It also allows me to most quickly find out what's most important to you today.

In this second gear, even if you have a long-term goal in mind, you often don't yet know exactly what part you want to focus on. So, this gear is your time to run through several things that are on your mind, but most importantly, express those things that are felt most deeply or impacting you the most.

As your coach, it's important that I write down a brief list of the topics you cover in your braindump so that I can repeat the list back to you when you're done speaking. By listing your topics back to you, you can either pick the one most important topic for the day or discover what connection the topics may have with each other, if any.

CHECKLIST

As your coach, here are the actions I take in second gear in order to explore your heart space, uncovering all of the things on your mind concerning your goals.

Of course, the following checklist items all happen within this gear, but they don't necessarily happen in the order that each checkbox is listed. And I don't have to address an item if it has already been directly addressed in an earlier conversation.

Second Gear Checklist (Destination Conversations)

- ☑ Explore multiple topics (braindump)
- ☑ Provide acknowledgments, validations, observations, and celebrations
- ☑ Allow silent pauses for processing
- ☑ Calibrate (discover client's tone of joy)
- ☑ Discover your motivators (if not done prior to conversation)
- ☑ Discover what you are tolerating in life right now
- ☑ Perform life inventory (if not done prior to conversation)
- ☑ Review how you feel or what you think about your life inventory

Second Gear Checklist (Next Stop Conversations)

- ☑ Explore multiple topics (braindump)
- ☑ Ask about completed homework and/or what they learned in the process
- ☑ Provide acknowledgments, validations, observations, and celebrations
- ☑ Allow silent pauses for processing

TECHNIQUES AND TOOLS

Clarity

As you learned earlier in this book, each coaching conversation accomplishes two things - first, clarity, and afterward, Action.

Getting clarity is the purpose of first, second, third, and fourth gears. As I shift upward in our conversation from first to fourth gears, the more clarity you gain.

In other words, first gear is the lowest grade of clarity; it's only about getting clear on coaching basics. Second gear is a braindump - getting clear on all the wants and don't-wants that are on your mind at the moment. Third gear is about getting clarity on one single point of focus that is most important to you at the time of our conversation. And fourth gear crowns that focus by giving it a name.

To get clarity is to name what it is that you truly want, and then, to be able to see in your mind and feel in your chest the reward of obtaining it.

Sometimes people know what they want, but they don't have someone to keep them accountable and encouraged to obtain it. One of the great roles of a coach is to keep you accountable and encouraged to pursue it.

I often find that people once knew what they want, but someone or something long ago stopped them from believing they could have it and, defeated, they let go of its pursuit. Other times, people honestly don't know exactly what they want in life because no one has asked them the right questions or given them the right exercises to discover it.

If you cannot see or feel a reward in what you do, your enthusiasm begins to wane, and the likelihood of completion begins to diminish. This likelihood is rooted in brain chemistry - our brain's wiring favors reward-driven actions. Without some form of reward, we feel a sense of loss.

Clarity also requires a feeling of safety. I learned years ago that when we feel ourselves in a state of fear, the brain's decision-making and higher-order thinking can become impaired. During fear states, the brain is too busy prioritizing survival functions to think clearly.

In fear state, the brain cannot think clearly, so as your coach, I aim to ensure a safe place for you to unravel your thoughts without the neurological restrictions of fear.

Heart Space

There's a motivational meme that I saw and saved years ago that I treasure dearly, and it is one way for me to illustrate my idea of "heart space." The meme shows a scientific illustration of two human organs.

On top, it shows what looks like a medical book drawing of a brain with "Figure 1" written underneath it.

Further down, it shows what looks like another medical illustration of a human heart with "Figure 2" written underneath it.

Under "Figure 1," it reads "This is your brain. Inside are the things worth living by."

Under "Figure 2," it reads "This is your heart. Inside are the things worth dying for."

The spirit of that meme powerfully communicates the impact of what I call "heart space." While the brain provides wisdom worth living by – or even a type of "common sense," the heart provides the values worth dying for - or things that might sometimes make no sense to others.

In a coaching conversation, the point of the second gear is to begin to scratch the surface of topics that, for you, are "worth dying for."

These topics may be a mixture of positive and negative emotions. The list may include a bunch of things you *don't want* and *do want*.

To know what you want and don't want, it requires that you use your brain, but that you also have capacity to feel your emotions.

Heart space refers to the place in your body where you sense your emotions happening, usually in your chest or abdomen.

Head space and heart space work together, but for some reason, it's often harder for people to access heart space. *Head space* refers to the place in your skull where you record information and calculate it. It's the physical place in your body where non-emotional observation and logical decision-making happens.

Finding heart space means arriving at a point in a conversation where you can sense that you're feeling or speaking with emotion, not with logic alone.

In first gear, you were probably talking mostly in head space to confirm logistics, such as the time frame for the conversation today and any other general facts. Maybe you also just jumped on our call right after a long day at work, where you felt completely disconnected from emotion. However, in second gear, we start accessing and sorting out what's going on in your heart space.

When I ask you questions, your emotionally-aware answers will have more power and impact on your life than a purely logical answer. Heart space is about identifying what you personally value. By accessing both spaces, I can help you make decisions that are both wise and genuinely valuable to you.

I emphasize heart space in this gear because logical ideas without emotions attached to them tend to have little or no long-term value in our lives. You're more likely to give up quickly when your emotions are not in it.

Purely logical goals may potentially develop emotional value for you at some point, but, when it comes to coaching, we look for goals that also have meaningful emotional value attached to it, and that value comes from heart space.

Both heart space and head space work together in coaching, but heart space is where you store those things that are most uniquely meaningful to you, so that is where we seek to stay in every conversation and every decision.

Scenario to demonstrate heart space

Client: *I'm so nervous and don't know what to say or do in my meeting with everyone on Monday. I wrote down a bunch of notes, but there are so many random things I wrote and they are plain boring, and I feel anxious about the whole thing. There's too much going on in my head!*

Coach: *What do you think if we try a coaching technique right now to help you out?*

Client: *Yeah, okay.*

Coach: *Imagine a distinction between your head and heart. Speaking logically is led by what I call headspace, which refers to the physical place in your head and brain where you calculate things.*

What you have to say emotionally comes from what I call heart space, referring to the physical place in your chest near your heart where you sense emotions.

Now, imagine if you could speak powerfully from heart space for your meeting. What would you say if you spoke more powerfully from heart space?

Client: *Wow, okay. Well, I would probably be far more honest and probably more interesting to listen to in the meeting if I did speak from that place.*

Coach: *What else?*

Client: *I'd get straight to it and bring up the real core issue we're all facing. I'd ask everyone in the room for ideas on how to address it so that we can all find a resolution together. Then, in that process, I think everything else would just fall into place. You know what? That's a legitimate agenda right there. I can brainstorm ideas with the group for a few minutes to see what they have in mind.*

Life Inventory

A life inventory is formal coaching exercise where you measure your satisfaction and health in all areas of your life. Just as a checkup at the doctor's office will tell you what needs attention, so does the life inventory.

When getting clarity on a long-term goal and planning your next steps, it's important for that goal to be viewed within the context of other areas of your life. Doing that helps you to ensure that the goal you work toward is one that really matters the most to you.

By doing the life inventory, you make sure that change you're about to make is one that fits into the story of your life and it is truly a destination worthy of driving toward at this time.

There are two effective ways to do your life inventory, either in a live destination conversation with me, or as a form that you fill in by yourself. When it's in a live conversation, it's done in second gear.

The life inventory uncovers topics that may impact your well-being and your ability to make the changes you want to make. So, just as we need a semi-annual or annual checkup at the doctor's office, the life inventory typically needs to happen every six months to a year.

You don't go to a doctor just once for a checkup; rather, you go on a regular basis. Likewise, levels of health and satisfaction will change during different seasons of life, and, as times change, so will your scores.

So, if we work together for more than six months, I may bring up your life inventory again.

How do you do a life inventory?

If you look back in your diary to question number 6 in Chapter 6's Exercise, you'll see that you assigned scores to twelve areas in your life. *That was your life inventory.*

I could either give you a form to fill in prior to our live conversation or I can ask you all twelve questions live in our first destination conversation.

A life inventory asks you to give a score between 1 (one) and 10 (ten) to represent how satisfied you feel about each of the twelve areas of life. A score of 1 means that it couldn't be any worse, and a score of 10 means it couldn't be any better.

- Body health (including medical health and fitness)

- Financial health
- Restful activities (low energy downtime, reclining, relaxing, chillout activities)
- Playful activities (having fun, energizing activities, celebrating - whether big or small)
- Emotions and thought life
- Occupation (career, trade, and business)
- Discovery (learning, novelty, and exploration)
- Time management (prioritization, scheduling, and calendar
- Self-view (how you view yourself and self-esteem)
- Worldview (Spiritual, religious, intellectual, moral, or philosophical life)
- Environments at work, home, and anywhere in between (lighting, furniture, space, noise, etc.)
- Human relationships (including friendship, intimate partnership, family, professional, political, or any other)

Stopping to evaluate a birds-eye view of your life can help you prioritize what's important to you, and it can also help you take more motivated action.

Another way to look at the life inventory is to understand it as an all-of-life health check-up on your self-care. We often neglect our own basic needs and desires. When many people and things demand our time and attention, our very foundation for helping everyone else often begins to crack. Lack of self-care eventually results in losing our own health in some or many forms.

For example, body health is the first item on the list. For me, body health involves getting enough hours of sleep, getting all of my nutritional needs, drinking enough water, getting exercise, practicing good hygiene to avoid illness, and so much more. If this ingredient of self-care isn't addressed properly, it can slow me down or completely stop me from chasing my goal.

Are there other kinds of life inventories?

Yes, there are more specific forms of the life inventories that can be performed when we need to focus on a particular area of life.

For example, if you want to focus your coaching experience on human relationships, I may use a form of the life inventory that applies specifically to all the areas of human relationships. As the author of *The Boundaries Health Check*, I designed a type of life inventory that quantifies and tracks the health of any of your human relationships.

If I coach you as a Business Coach, I may use a form of the life inventory designed for all the areas of your business.

So, yes, you can take any of the twelve areas of life and design a life inventory for each if you felt it would help you.

Braindump

When you get on a coaching call with me as your coach, you might have a long list of things going through your mind. It helps to "think out loud" and talk through all those things until you find the most pressing matter to discuss. Braindumping is the term for simply unloading all your thoughts in no particular order and with no expectations or judgment.

A good coach will keep track of the time that you scheduled and will help you reign in your braindump if needed.

On the other hand, you may get on a coaching call and know right away what you want from the day's session; so, you won't need a braindump.

When I speak with my own personal coach, my braindumps are essential for me. They're like turning my pocketbook upside down on the table in order to find my money buried underneath all the tissues, wrappers, headphones, sunblock bottle, lip-gloss, and shopping lists.

Braindumping is also like throwing all my clean clothes onto the bed to sort out what I want to wear today.

Calibrate

The general definition of "calibrate" is to check or adjust something by comparison with a standard.

In coaching, calibrating is to check or adjust your level of motivation by comparison with a standard that you set for me.

As your coach, I ask questions to discover what you *sound like* when you're happy, motivated, or feeling meaningful. Once I establish what *that* sounds like, I can start to make adjustments or "calibrate" your direction of decision-making in order to keep you aligned with what helps you feel happy, motivated, or meaningful.

Our coaching relationship relies on my ability to learn about you over time and identify your unique expressions of joy, happiness, meaningfulness, or motivation.

And what's a great way to calibrate? Asking you about one of the happiest times in your life helps me hear what you sound like when you're feeling good about something. Asking you about your greatest values helps me learn what it sounds like when you're feeling like life is meaningful.

By learning your tones of voice and patterns, I am calibrating, which means I can more confidently make observations such as, "Your voice sounded happier when you said that. What does that mean for you?"

Asking questions about what you're tolerating in life helps me hear what you sound like when you're *not* happy or *not* satisfied with something.

By asking *both* - your happiest moment and what you're tolerating - helps me contrast your tones of voice. Asking these two questions close together also helps you think about what you really want to change in your life.

I learn your patterns better over time throughout our coaching conversations. However, calibrating questions are most important in the destination conversation and in second gear, because it lays down a solid foundation for whatever short-term or long-term goal you are designing at that time.

Homework

The term "homework" shows up in the Next Stop Conversation Checklist (in second gear), and it refers to any work, effort, challenge, or exercise that you planned in the previous coaching conversation.

All professional coaching conversations end with some form of an action that a client designs with their coach in order to move forward toward their goal. Some clients may not like the word "homework" because it sounds like a dreaded school assignment, as opposed to sounding (more accurately) like a motivated next step toward a person's dreams and goals!

So, although most professional coaches call it "homework," feel free to call it something more friendly like accomplishment, movement forward, exercise, challenge, or most simply your "next step."

Remember, without designing an action of some kind, it's not coaching and it's not moving forward.

Authoring

Authoring is about framing or phrasing your situation to make you the author of your own story.

I intentionally frame a question or observation in a way that highlights that *you are the author of your choices*. I do this to put a sense of power back into your hands when you're in a situation where you might feel a loss of control.

Authoring questions puts the ball into your court. As your coach, I may ask, "What led you to choose that?" or "What did you learn from making that decision?" or "How did you fix this kind of situation in the past?"

Scenario demonstrating authoring

Client: *I'm feeling confused about the career path I'm on. When I did my Master of Event Management, I was pretty certain I wanted to pursue this career path. I'm not so sure now. I simply don't really like my job at all.*

Coach: *What made you choose this career path?*

Client: *Well, I like planning and organizing and knew I would like looking after the logistics. Plus, I thought it would be fun.*

Coach: *How much planning and organizing do you do in your current job?*

Client: *I think that's the problem. I'm really only doing the legwork for my manager, and not the amount of planning and organizing I want.*

Coach: *If you could do anything to make this situation better, what would you do?*

Client: *I would ask my boss for more planning and organizing tasks because it's my passion, and, well, if she doesn't like it, I can look to move on to another job that suits me better.*

Coach: *Based on that, what kind of action would you like to take between now and our next conversation?*

Client: *I will have a talk with her and see what she says. That will be a defining moment!*

Acknowledgments, Validations, and Observations

The purposes of providing you my acknowledgements, validations, and observations are to affirm that all your thoughts and feelings matter (whether negative or positive), that you are valuable, and that you are being fully heard.

Acknowledgements are recognizing your effort or achievement. For example, "You put hard work into this project," or "You made a step forward, despite the obstacles."

Observations are noting factual behaviors, measurable actions, or visible or audible differences. For example, "I notice your voice sounds more light-hearted now that you completed that task you originally didn't want to do," or "You completed three to-do items this week."

Validations: Affirming someone's feelings or experiences. For example, "It's completely normal to feel stress about this kind of a situation," or "It's normal for people who do great things to experience great obstacles."

Scenario to demonstrate acknowledgements, validations, and observations

Client: *I am so upset about this situation at work. It's too frustrating to even deal with. I just want to grab my boss by the shoulders and shake him! I work so hard, and he doesn't even notice it.*

Coach: *Your frustration makes sense. You put so much hard work into this project, and you don't feel noticed for it.*

Client: *Thank you. Yes. It feels good hearing someone acknowledge how I feel without judgement.*

Celebrations

The purpose of celebrating is to create momentum.

Celebrating even the tiniest win creates a sense of momentum. And making a habit of celebrating small wins over time creates unexpectedly powerful results. If you look into professional research in this subject, you will find overwhelming evidence that "small wins" are one of the key ingredients for the most effective change.

Small wins are important in every area of life, including at work. A study of nearly 12,000 diary entries provided by 238 employees in seven companies showed that minor victories turned out to be nearly as effective as major breakthroughs. One of the authors of the study wrote, "We found that 28 percent of small events of all kinds had a major impact on inner work life."[12]

Celebrating wins - big or small - is a secret to long-term success. Celebrating a win can be as small as buying a special coffee or as big as throwing a lavish party.

Whether it's only me applauding your win and/or you rewarding your effort through a small action, the technique of celebrating helps you know that all forms of effort and achievements matter, deserve recognition, and are being fully heard by me as the coach.

Scenario to demonstrate celebrations

Coach: *So, what's happened since our last conversation?*

Client: *I've done some more research about my idea of starting a not-for-profit. I found a few interesting points. Otherwise, things are still kind of the same at work, still not enjoying it. But the other day, I had a discussion with my boss' boss. We actually talked about not-for-profits. I told him my idea and vision for a not-for-profit because he's got a few successful ones. He has the same passion as me; it's kind of funny. I can feel it. He was very intrigued and said that if I had questions, I could ask him anytime for help or advice. But that's beside the point. I've really focused my research on my target market this week. I started to get a clearer idea, but I'm still in between two options.*

Coach: *Before we continue, I hear four wins to celebrate. First, congratulations for passionately communicating your vision for your business when, in the past, you had difficulties doing so. Second, you found yourself in a conversation with a new resource of wisdom to help you with your not-for-profit idea. Third, you received positive feedback. Fourth, congrats on being invited for some mentoring!*

Client: *Oh, okay! Hm. I didn't see it like that, but I do now. Wow. I do have some small wins to there.*

Brainstorming

In our conversations, there may be times when I hit pause to ask you how helpful it may or may not be to have a brainstorm session.

Brainstorming is a creative exercise that usually results in a new direction, perspective, or solution you haven't thought of before. When I brainstorm with a client, I follow five basic rules:

Rule #1 No Judgement Zone
You agree not to judge any of your ideas during brainstorming. The magic of brainstorming is that, even if you think something is an outrageous or boring idea, it could spark a brilliant one. I make sure you know that all ideas are needed.

Rule #2 Quantity Over Quality
Come up with as many ideas as possible - ideas of all size and quality. The more ideas you have to work with, the better the chance is for something wonderfully unexpected.

Rule #3 Evolve Ideas
If you come up with an idea, you might continue to build on it further or change it into something strange or different or new, even if it seems odd at first.

Rule #4 Stay Wild
Keep an open mind. It's important that I encourage you to say even those things that you may be embarrassed to say. It's best to stay *outside the box* to trigger as much creativity as possible.

Rule #5 Record Everything
Write down all of your ideas, whether they are big or small, meaningful, or ridiculous. This is part of the magic that triggers new thoughts and solutions, either immediately or hours or days later.

COACHING QUESTIONS

Second gear requires the exploration of various topics to see what's going on and to give your next step a firm foundation and context.

When we speak for the first time in a destination conversation, second gear is when we go through the life inventory, discover your motivators (see Chapter 5), and/or discover what you might be tolerating in life right now.

Ideally, we go through all of those in second gear in our first conversation, but it may depend on what we may have already covered prior to the conversation.

In a next stop conversation, the topics we cover in second gear are whatever is on your mind and what's happened since our last conversation.

Here below are some examples of coaching questions that I might ask in order to start accessing your heart space.

Second Gear Questions (Destination Conversations)

Questions to Calibrate
- What is one of the happiest moments of your life? Just one short story.
- What is one of the funniest moments of your life? Just one short story.
- What is one thing that you feel proud to have done in your life? It can be big or small.
- When you look back on your life, what event or events brought you the most joy?
- Who in your life brings you the most joy? These can be people you know personally or people who have positively impacted you but you haven't met.

Questions to Discover Your Tolerations
- When you look at your life inventory, what are you tolerating the most?
- What are you tolerating at this time in your life?
- What is it costing you to keep tolerating [insert what you said you are tolerating]?

- What will it cost you if you do nothing about it?
- What is stopping you from accomplishing what you want to achieve in life?

Questions That Help Find Your Heart Space
- Imagine you could make your life perfect; what would you change?
- What is something you really want in life but you don't tell many people?
- If your life was a book and you were the only author of that book, how would you want that story to go?
- Who do you want to be in general?
- What do you want to achieve during your life?
- Imagine you are 99 years old. What do you want to have done that would make you feel proud?
- What does success look like for you?
- What does success feel like for you?
- What do you feel most passionate about right now?
- What is missing from your life right now?
- What percentage of that answer comes from your heart space and how much comes from head space?
- If you spoke completely from your heart space, what would you say?
- What else would you like to say about that?
- What else can you tell me about that?
- What if you do?
- What if you don't?
- What could you do if it doesn't work out the way you wish?

Questions to Review Life Inventory
- What stands out to you the most from your life inventory?
- Which of your life inventory scores make the biggest difference in your life?

Second Gear Questions (Next Stop Conversations)

Explore Multiple Topics (Braindump)
- How've you been since we last chatted?
- How important is [insert your destination] to you today?
- What are some highlights or lowlights since our last conversation?
- So, how do you feel at the moment?
- What's on your mind?
- What else?
- How did you do with [insert goal from our last conversation]?
- What worked for you and what didn't work?
- What do you feel most proud of?
- How have you celebrated or how are you going to celebrate that win?
- What decision or attitude made that win possible?
- How happy are you with what you just said?
- How would it feel to fail after trying vs. never trying at all?
- What have you learned about yourself in the process?

ICF CORE COMPETENCIES

As you can see from the checklist and the coaching questions for this chapter, second gear demonstrates quite a few of ICF's Core Competencies, including:

- Establishing Trust and Intimacy
- Coaching Presence
- Asking Powerful Questions
- Active Listening
- Creating Awareness
- Managing Progress and Accountability

Establishing Trust and Intimacy

By giving you the safe space to share whatever is on your mind and by helping you understand what you have learned about yourself in the process, it's one of the ways that second gear allows for the "genuine concern for [your] welfare and future."

Coaching Presence

In one conversation you may spend a large amount of time "braindumping" in second gear, while other conversations you may be so clear on what you want that we go straight from first to third gear. So, I'm present and flexible during the coaching process or "dancing in the moment" by being ready to shift to any gear at any time.

Asking Powerful Questions

A focus on life inventory, calibrating, motivators, tolerations, and a safe space for braindumping will "reveal the information needed for the maximum benefit" for the client.

Active Listening

During a braindump, I listen to you "vent or clear the situation without judgment or attachment." I ask for more information when I believe it would help you gain more clarity. And when I calibrate, I'm starting to distinguish "between the words, the tone of voice, and the body language" you express so that I understand you more clearly as we move forward.

Creating Awareness

As we move into heart space, I aim to create "greater understanding, awareness, and clarity," no matter what you're discussing. I may ask you what the connection between two items is in your braindump or help you to see a strength that you exhibited in a situation. Both help you become more aware of yourself and what you want.

Managing Progress and Accountability

Finally, an important aspect of second gear in every next stop conversation we have, is that I demonstrate "follow-through by asking [you] about those actions that [you] committed to do during the previous conversation(s)." If you've accomplished your goal, I acknowledge your success and celebrate with you. If you did not complete your action, it's my job to ask how it may be done differently next time or ask what you've learned about yourself. The purpose is not to be your taskmaster but to keep you celebrating your wins and accountable to your goa

Exercise (Chapter 10)

In your diary, write today's date and "Chapter 10" on top of the page.

Here are some reflections that integrate a few of the ideas that you learned in this chapter.

EARN 1 POINT

1. Following the rules of "brainstorming" as described in this chapter, write out a creative list of several different ways that you might reach your long-term goal. Come up with at least three to five, but list more you wish.

For example, my long-term goal (destination) might be to move to a new city. So, in my brainstorm, I might list creative ways that I might reach that goal, such as: (1) move with my best friend, (2) relocate there through my job, (3) save up money then find a place and job when I arrive there, or (4) visit a few times to find a place and job then move there.

EARN 1 POINT

2. Now, read the brainstorm list that you wrote down in question number 1 above.

Similar to the "calibration" technique, you're going to check your own sense of happiness, satisfaction, or meaningfulness. Out of the answers you listed in your brainstorm above, pick the one that makes you feel the *most* motivated. There is no right or wrong answer.

Check your own internal emotional response as you read each idea that you wrote. Then, write down your top pick as your answer to this question.

EARN 1 POINT

3. On a scale of 1 to 10, with "1" meaning you *couldn't be any less* honest and "10" meaning you *could not be any more* honest, how honest were you with yourself in both of your answers above (question number 1 and question number 2)?

Write down your score.

MAXIMUM POINTS EARNED FOR THIS CHAPTER

You earn 1 point for completing each of the 3 questions above for a maximum of 3 points.

Count the number of points you completed and write down the total number on your Scoreboard, as described in Exercise Chapter 1.

CHAPTER 11, THIRD GEAR - FIND THE FIRE

DEFINITION

In third gear, we sort out the topics you mentioned in second gear in order to find which one matters the most to you. I look for the one most important topic that gives you energy, meaning, and desire, which is why I use the metaphor of a fire.

This fire represents what you have the most motivation or passion for right now, based on all the things you talked about in first and second gear.

Sometimes, you'll come to the coaching conversation already fired up with an idea; you'll speed straight through second gear and quickly into third, telling me right away what you would like to get from the coaching conversation. Other times, you may be cruising in second gear for a while until we find what we're looking for.

CHECKLIST

Third Gear Checklist (Destination Conversations)

- Find one most passionate change to make in any area of life (aka a "destination")
- Confirm what the change feels, looks, and sounds like
- Confirm how well it aligns with your motivators
- Confirm how that change would be different than your current experience
- Allow silent pauses for processing
- Identify what it will cost if you don't make this change

Third Gear Checklist (Next Stop Conversations)

- Find one most passionate change or action to complete between now and our next conversation (aka a "next stop")
- Confirm what the change feels, looks, and sounds like
- Confirm how well it aligns with your motivators
- Confirm what would be different than your current experience
- Identify how this change progresses the journey to your destination
- Allow silent pauses for processing
- Identify what it will cost if you don't take this next step

TECHNIQUES AND TOOLS

Several of the following coaching techniques and tools help you break free from restricted or fear-driven thinking, so that you can more easily identify what deeply matters to you.

To do this, I help you use your imagination to experience, as richly as possible, the impact of achieving your goal, and what that might look and feel like physically and emotionally. I also help you recognize how well your goal aligns with your motivators so that you can feel more assured that your goal also aligns with your genuine sense of self and values.

Destination

In third gear of our very first coaching conversation, we identify a destination.

"Destination" refers to the long-term goal you decide to work on in our coaching relationship. Of course, after you reach your destination, we can design a new one, but as your coach, I will hold you accountable to one destination until you reach it.

As a client, it's ultimately your choice as to the length of time meant by "long term goal." Your destination may be five years, five months, or five weeks.

Currently, the average length of "long term" for a coaching client is six months, but what "long term" means to you will vary depending on your life's circumstances.

Anything more than one year often makes clients lose motivation because it seems too far beyond grasp or they might expect life circumstances to change in that time frame. For other clients, five to ten years can seem like an easy time frame.

In your life, what's the farthest ahead that you can *reasonably* and *comfortably* see? Is it weeks, months, years, or decades? That is what "long term" means for you.

Here are some random and general examples of destinations that someone may decide to work toward.

- Start a career in a creative industry by the end of next year.
- Experience romance daily in my relationship with my partner between now and the end of summer.
- Launch a business within the next two years.
- Move to a new town by next month.
- Lock down spending in order to save a $45,000 deposit by December of next year.
- Over two months, go hang out once a week in places where singles hangout.

Next Stop

Your next stop is simply your *next step* of action toward your destination, and it is something you believe you can complete either within the next seven days or before our next coaching conversation, whichever comes first.

In Chapter 7's exercise, you've already experienced a conversation format that is dedicated to designing a next stop.

Here are some random or general examples of next stops that a person may decide to work toward:

- Apply for the Adobe Creative Suite training program on Friday before work. [A next stop toward the destination of a career change.]
- Shop lingerie catalogues during my lunch break and pick out one item that makes me feel sexy. [A next stop toward the destination of experiencing romance in a relationship.]
- Bring my laptop to a cafe on Saturday to research which state is the best to register my business. [A next stop toward the destination of launching a business.]
- Look at a map to find which towns have the best public transport. [A next stop toward the destination of moving to a new town.]

- Review current spending to see what unnecessary subscriptions can be cancelled. [A next stop toward the destination of locking down spending.]
- Research and create a list of events and places where singles hang out locally. [A next stop toward the destination of hanging out weekly with singles.]

Fast Forwarding

When you desire something that you don't tangibly have in hand just yet, "fast forwarding" is a coaching technique that helps you mentally prepare yourself to get it.

Fast forwarding is a mental exercise where, only in your mind, you take anywhere from one minute to several minutes experiencing the event and feeling the achievement in your imagination, as if you've arrived in the future and it's happening right now.

It's like fast forwarding a video of your life to the future to watch and listen to the accomplishment of the goal.

If you perform this coaching technique on your own, then it's helpful to set a timer, but whether you do it alone or with your coach, in that time, its effectiveness will depend on whether or not you can intentionally *feel the emotions* that accompany the completion of the event or achievement.

Imagine the kind of new thoughts you would have in that moment, how others would see you differently, how you would see yourself differently, and any changes in what you might hear, see, smell, taste, or touch in the environment in those moments.

Upon the "actual" physical completion of the goal in "real life," you may or may not end up feeling those same emotions that you imagined in this exercise; your real-life feelings may be better, the same, or different. However, feeling something in your imagination is essential to this technique being effective.

Part of the imagined "movie" is visualizing what your hands or skin is touching, or what (or who) you're hearing, or what (or who) you're seeing.

You visualize and feel and sense as much as you can, as long as it feels *good*.

There are many other related techniques to fast forwarding. Some psychologists call it a "mental rehearsal," and others call it "visualization." The reason why I named it "fast forwarding" is because it is like pressing the "fast forward" button on a recording to skip ahead to the event or part that you need to see.

The key is this. When you make it a habit to fast forward to the achievement with your full imagination, it becomes much easier and more motivating to achieve it and you'll more quickly recognize opportunities "in real life" that bring you closer toward it.

In an upcoming chapter, I introduce a similar technique that I call "rewinding," in which you replay a behavior or action of yours from your past as though you had completed it to your satisfaction. Rewinding is replaying an event in the past that you were unhappy about but you re-imagine it as if you had acted, spoke, behaved, or made a decision in the way that you would have desired to.

Both mental rehearsal techniques of fast forwarding and rewinding can powerfully help your brain to make decisions and take actions that more closely align with who you want to be and where you want to go in life.

They are ways to better prepare you for the future.

Mental rehearsal techniques aren't only fun exercises, but they are scientifically proven methods to make a serious change in your life. I like how Frank Niles, Ph.D. said it in the Huffington Post.

Visualization should not be confused with the "think it and you will be it" advice peddled by popular self-help gurus. It is not a gimmick, nor does it involve dreaming or hoping for a better future. Rather, visualization is a well-developed method of performance improvement supported by substantial scientific evidence and used by successful people across a range of fields. [13]

The Washington Post also published an article describing how Olympic athletes use visualization with amazing results. [14]

In a study conducted by Guang Yue, an exercise physiologist at the Cleveland Clinic Foundation, after 12 weeks of only visualizing weight training, the subjects of the study showed a 13.5% increase in strength. [15]

As mentioned on Psychology Today, mental rehearsal or visualization has been a key component for World Champion Golfers like Jack Nicklaus and Tiger Woods as well as for heavyweight champion Muhammad Ali. [16]

When you use the visualizing technique of "fast forwarding," you take time feeling and describing every detail as if it has already happened, and it becomes even more potent with the more detail that you include. Here's an example in the context of a personal coaching conversation.

Scenario to demonstrate fast forwarding

Coach: *What do you think about doing a very short exercise called fast forwarding? It basically walks you through a scene in your life after you've reached your goal.*

Client: *Yeah, that's fine.*

Coach: *Okay, let's pretend that we were able to stop time right now and, like watching a video of your life, we now fast forward to the point in the future when you've achieved your goal. So, we have now fast forwarded, and right now, we are in the future. Picture yourself having achieved it. Can you see it in your mind?*

Client: *Yes, I see it.*

Coach: *What do you see, hear, taste, touch, say, or observe that is now different in your life? Speak in the present tense as if it is happening right now.*

Client: *Oh, wow. Well, I see smiles on my kids' faces and hear them laugh. I am able to hug them and tell them how much I love them. I feel so loved.*

Coach: *What kind of new thoughts do you have, now that you have achieved it?*

Client: *I'm thinking of how it was hard but it was all worthwhile, all that work and investment. I'm thinking how I can now look forward to focusing on other areas of my life.*

Coach: *What, if anything, are other people saying?*

Client: *My kids are saying thank you. My good friend is saying "wow, finally."*

Coach: *What other thoughts do you have?*

Client: *This is energizing.*

Role Play

Role playing in coaching is a creative technique that incorporates you and/or others as "make believe" characters to allow your mind to more creatively and playfully overcome mental obstacles, inner self-conflict, conflict with another person, or confusion.

In role playing, I propose a scenario using imaginary people or characters and make believe character traits. Then I ask you to imagine that character or character element and I ask questions about it.

Over the years, it sounds like child's play and yet it has amazed me time and time again how powerfully and frequently this fun technique results in mature and creative solutions. First, you think of the wild or imaginative solution through the exercise, but then afterwards, it somehow can inspire you to realize a practical and realistic one.

Here are some of my favorite role plays:

Magic Wand

This is a popular coaching tool, where I ask you to pretend that you own a magic wand that gives you full power to do anything and everything. Then I ask, "If you could wave your magic wand, what would you make happen in this situation?"

A client who faced declining sales might imagine waving their magic wand to create a bustling store with eager customers, and that might inspire or spark a new marketing strategy. A partner feeling unattractive might imagine waving their magic wand to create a super sexy body, and that might inspire or spark the idea to start healthier diet habits.

Twos

This works well if you start feeling a conflict within yourself between two opposing thoughts, ideas, options, or emotions. I would ask you to give a name to each of the two opposing thoughts, ideas, or emotions, and imagine each of them as characters sitting on their own next to each other talking. I would ask questions that allow the two characters to come to a place of peace, understanding, and agreement.

Here is an example of how this scenario would work:

Client: *I'm the problem. I'm a strict person. I'm bossy toward my husband and children. It's affecting my whole family. I feel like such a bad person. So bad.*

Coach: *How do you feel about trying out an imaginative exercise right now to help you sort this out?*

Client: Sure.

Coach: *Ok, when you say "bad person", what's a name that you can give that character?*

Client: *I don't know. Maybe call her Bad Susy.*

Coach: *Let's pretend Bad Susy is sitting on a chair next to Good Susy. In this situation, tell me what does Good Susy say to Bad Susy?*

Client: *Good Susy would ask Bad Susy to stop yelling. She would tell Bad Susy to try peacefully explaining to her family why it is important to her that they help her with home duties. Good Susy would also help Bad Susy to be more understanding and maybe not want everything done straight away.*

Coach: *What are your thoughts after hearing yourself say that?*

Client: *Hah, well, Good Susy does have a point about expecting everything straight away. Maybe Bad Susy can start to break things down into smaller pieces to make it more manageable.*

Perfect World

Here, I simply ask you to imagine a "perfect world" where no negative consequences exist and there are no limits. Then I'd ask, "In a perfect world, what would you do?" or "In a perfect world, what do you see?"

Even though we're using imagination, it's astonishing how often practical and realistic possibilities show up after this exercise.

For example, you may not see any options, and so as your coach, I ask "In a perfect world, what options would you have?" In your mind, limitations suddenly drop away, and you might respond with, "If the world was perfect, I'd know exactly *who to go to* for the answer. Oh wait. actually, now that I think about it, there is someone I haven't thought of to ask!"

I like to walk through an entirely imaginative "perfect world" scenario, but all too often a real-life solution shows up very quickly into the exercise. I often don't even get to finish it!

Gardener

When you're dealing with a situation in which you experience a lot of resistance, rejection, or disappointment, one role play that's fun and helpful might be the gardener.

This is where you imagine you are a gardener tasked to make something life-giving from this awful situation. I tell you that the resistance, rejection, or disappointment you feel has become magical fertilizer that you can use to grow something good or life-giving from the situation. So, I might ask, "If you could grow anything from this situation, what are a few things - big or small - you could possibly grow from this?"

Character Swap

In this scenario I ask you to pretend that you're either someone else in your life who you admire or you are a fictional character you love.

Then I ask you to tell me what that person would say to you or what that person would do in the situation. For example, I may ask you to think of someone you most admire in your life, and then I ask, "Imagine you are your [insert name of that person]. As [that person], what would you likely *think* about this situation?"

If you're stuck making a decision, this is also a helpful way to get unstuck. Simply ask, "Imagine you are [that person], what option would you likely go with?" The answer often sheds some light for you to make progress.

Silence (Allow Silent Pauses)

This is a simple technique that you will see on several of the checklists in this book. It seems so basic, but it is often tragically neglected.

Silence, as a coaching skill, refers to when I intentionally stop and wait after I ask you a question so that you can more thoroughly process the question, and it also refers to when I wait after an observation or after you speak, in case you have something more say. It may last a few seconds or many more, depending on the complexity of the topic.

In a casual *non-coaching* conversation, people jump in to speak as quickly as possible after the other person is done talking. In contrast, a proper coaching conversation gives you space to breath.

In that silent space of time, it allows for important mental and/or emotional processes to take place. It allows time to access your memory or creativity.

I am often also giving you space and time to process what you've already said, what I've said, or what I've asked.

Powerful realizations or decisions can come out of long waits of silence.

This skill is, perhaps, one of the most awkward to learn how to use, but it becomes one of the most powerfully simple techniques in coaching. It allows you the space that you need to come to your own surprising conclusions.

Sometimes, the space of silence can last so long that I will speak up to remind you that I'm still here on the phone letting you think it through.

Here is an example of how this scenario would work:

Client: *I don't know what to do. I really don't know.*

Coach: *What do you think would be your very first step to knowing?*

Client: *Well... (sigh) I... Well...*

Coach: *Take your time. I'll wait here while you think.*

(10 seconds of silence later...)

Coach: *I'm still here, take your time.*

Client: *Okay, I think I know now. I just thought of two people who can help. I'd forgotten that they were even possibilities.*

COACHING QUESTIONS

The following questions are examples of what I might ask in order to tick all the boxes required in third gear.

Third Gear Questions (Destination Conversations)

- How far ahead can you comfortably see in your life right now?
- How far ahead would you like to look into your life right now?
- When you look ahead into your life, what do you need the most?
- What goal will make your coaching experience the most worthwhile?
- In one sentence, what's your long-term goal?
- What would you change in your life to align yourself more closely with your motivator?
- What do you really, really want?
- What goal would you set for yourself if you knew you couldn't fail?
- What does your nervous system tell you about this?
- What are you most passionate about changing in your life right now?
- What would be the most meaningful and powerful thing you'd like to work on?
- What change would make the biggest difference in your life right now?
- If you had no fear of [insert what client fears], what would you do?
- What would you want to do if you knew for a fact you could not possibly fail?
- How does this align with your character strengths or motivators?
- What would really put a smile on your face right now?
- What connection may there be between ___ and ___?
- In one sentence, what words best describe your goal?
- We have explored a lot of ideas. In a few words, what do you really want?
- If you had only three seconds to say what you really want, what would you say?
- What words best describe what you're aiming for?
- If you could put that into only a few words, what would they be?
- What are you risking if you don't follow through with this?
- What's life going to be like in ___ months if you don't make it happen?
- What if you do nothing?

- When you reach your destination, what will you have gained?
- How might achieving this goal affect your life inventory scores?
- What might be different about your daily life after you accomplish this?

Third Gear Questions (Next Stop Conversations)

- What is most important for you to discuss today?
- What would be the most meaningful to work on today?
- What would be most productive to talk about today?
- What would be most meaningful to talk about today as you work toward [insert destination]?
- What would you like to accomplish today?
- What would you like to have accomplished by the end of our conversation today?
- Out of everything we've just talked about, what would you like to focus on today?
- What would you like to move forward with today?
- What would you like to make a move on today?
- What would mean the most for you to talk about today?
- How does this next step fit with your character strengths?
- How does this goal fit with your motivators?
- How well does this next step change align with your motivators?
- If you could achieve one thing in this phone call today, what would it be?
- What do you want to achieve in our call today?
- What would be most powerful for you to accomplish on this call?
- What would be the most helpful thing for you to get out of the next ___ minutes?
- In one sentence, what's your goal for today's conversation?
- How does this relate to your long-term goal?
- How does this help you with your long-term goal?

Questions for Visualizing, Role Playing, or Fast Forwarding

- What would it mean for you to accomplish what you said?
- Imagine you have achieved this goal. How would it feel or look like?
- How will life look or feel or sound different?
- How different will daily life look for you when that happens?
- What will you see around you that you're not seeing now?
- Once you achieve that goal, what will you be seeing differently that you don't see now?
- What will you be hearing differently that you don't hear now? That may be things people say, sounds in the environment, or something else.
- What, if anything, will you be tasting or eating differently that you don't now? That may be different foods you may be eating or something else.
- What will you be touching or holding differently that you don't touch or hold now?
- What will it feel like physically to achieve this?
- How may you be smelling or breathing differently than you do now? That may mean different air that you may be smelling, a different environment with different aromas, or it may mean that you're breathing more easily or more deeply, or something else.
- What will you be thinking differently that you don't think now?
- What will you be feeling differently that you don't feel now?

ICF CORE COMPETENCIES

Of ICF's list of Core Competencies, third gear most clearly utilizes:
- Powerful Questioning
- Creating Awareness
- Coaching Presence
- Active Listening

Powerful Questioning

Out of all gears, third gear is the most important one for "open-ended questions that create greater clarity, possibility or new learning." In my search for what makes you light up inside, I'm asking you "questions that move [you] toward what [you] desire, not questions that ask [you] to justify or look backward."

Creating Awareness

As I move through the checklist for this gear and ask questions, I'll be drilling ever deeper to bring new insights to the forefront of your mind. Finding what's most meaningful or passionate for you involves uncovering "the new thoughts, beliefs, perceptions, emotions, moods, etc. that strengthen [your] ability to take action and achieve what is important to [you]."

Coaching Presence

To be present, I have to be able to choose "in the moment what is most effective" to identify your most meaningful or most passionate goal, and based on your response, I choose which tools and techniques will fan that fire.

Active Listening

I'm listening for positive and strong emotional responses in order to uncover what you're most passionate about. I aim to be the one who "encourages, accepts, explores and reinforces [your] expression of feelings, perceptions, concerns, beliefs, suggestions, etc."

Exercise (Chapter 11)

In your diary, write today's date and "Chapter 11" on top of the page.

EARN 1 POINT

1. Think of your current destination (long-term goal). Now, pick one obstacle that stands in the way between you and your long-term goal. Then, choose one of the character "role play" techniques described in this chapter, and use it to either fully resolve the obstacle or lessen the strength that it has.

First, write down which role play technique you wish to use, and then in one paragraph or two, write out the entire role play to coach yourself through that obstacle.

EARN 1 POINT

2. Think of your current destination. We're going to use the "fast forward" technique to imagine you achieving it.

Imagine you have just achieved it. You have reached your long-term goal. What are some new or different thoughts you have, now that you achieved it? In approximately one paragraph, go through as many senses to describe the scene of your achievement.

EARN 1 POINT

3. Continuing with the fast forward technique in question number 2 above, let's imagine that you have just achieved your long-term goal.

In one or two sentences, how might others see you differently now? Also, how do *you see yourself* differently, now that you've achieved it?

MAXIMUM POINTS EARNED FOR THIS CHAPTER

You earn 1 point for answering each of the questions above for a maximum of 3 points.

Count the number of points you completed and write down the total number on your Scoreboard, as described in Exercise Chapter 1.

CHAPTER 12, FOURTH GEAR - WRITE THE WORDS

DEFINITION

In fourth gear, I find the "write" words. That's an intentional pun.

What I mean is that, in this gear, I write down your exact words to describe your goal, not my words. Your words are the "right words."

Here in fourth gear, writing down your exact words to name your goal will best prepare us to create the best action in fifth gear.

In this fourth gear, I am only looking for a string of roughly one to six words that describe your goal, like a movie or book title. Once I have it, we move on to fifth gear.

This fourth gear and the first gear are typically the quickest gears, since they're straight to the point.

At this point in the conversation, we are at the very end of the process of getting clarity in the conversation, and so in this gear, I confirm that I have the correct key words to describe your goal. I'll use these key words in future conversations, until you arrive at your destination.

One right or wrong word in your goal can have a major and impactful difference on your trajectory. One word can act like the small rudder on a ship - steering you in what ends up being a completely different direction over time.

The right word can also be compared to one strong spice in a dish - making it completely great or wrecking the whole thing.

So, in this gear, we zero in on what string of words fan your fire and keep you headed in your intended direction. You may already know those words, and so it's easy for me as your coach to write them down. Other times, we may need some time to settle on what fits best for you.

They key is that the words are yours, not mine.

CHECKLIST

The fourth gear checklist remains the same for all destination and next stop conversations.

- [x] Type or write client's exact word or phrase for their goal
- [x] Repeat word or phrase back to them
- [x] Allow silent pauses for processing

TECHNIQUES AND TOOLS

Note Taking

Taking notes is helpful for me all throughout the conversation, but it's most important for me to do it in here in fourth gear so that I can write it down and keep you accountable to it over time.

As your coach, the goal of note taking is to help me remember key things you've said in the conversation so that I can use your own words to help you get clarity and take action. As a professional coach with an obligation to codes of conduct, I also like to let you know that these notes are kept confidential.

Note taking might involve me writing down key words or phrases as you speak so I can echo them back to you, or, during a braindump, it may involve me writing a list of things you may have been speaking about so that I can read them back to you.

However, note taking is most important in fourth gear so that I can remember your exact names for your destination and your next stop(s).

Here are some of the most common notes that I take, as I listen to you:

- Your scores from any and all scaling questions throughout our coaching conversations
- Your destination (long-term goal)
- Your next stop (short-term goal)
- Your motivators (to use ongoing in our coaching conversations)
- Your reset buttons (we'll discuss this later in this book, in neutral gear)
- Your big and small wins (so I can remind you of them in later conversations or at future points)
- Any meaningful phrases you say that relate to your goal
- Any "Aha!" moments of self-learning or self-discovery (so that we can celebrate them)

Echoing

Hearing your own words echo back to you in natural settings like a canyon or mountain can feel awe-inspiring. There can also be something meditative about hearing your own voice return back to you in large spaces.

Likewise in a coaching conversation, when you're reflecting on the depths of your own needs or wishes, hearing your coach repeat back something you've said can have a similar effect.

To "echo" in a coaching conversation is simply the act of repeating back to you what you just said so that you can hear differently. Hearing your exact words spoken back to you can be like hearing a familiar song sung by a new artist. It gives you a different and new view of the "lyrics" that might help give you some insight or color to what you previously thought.

Echoing requires that I use your words exactly so that you can reflect more deeply on them. I don't change a single word you've said to me.

When I'm able to repeat back what you said to me, I'm also showing you that I'm with you, listening, and hearing you. It helps build our coaching relationship.

Scenario demonstrating echoing

Client: *It's difficult to decide because I love him so very much, but I have other major responsibilities. I don't know what to do.*

Coach: *"I love him so very much, but I have other major responsibilities." When you hear me repeat that, what do you think?*

Client: *I'm not normally this lovey-dovey. It makes me realize how important he is to me, and I honestly can't even remember when the last time was that I said that about anyone at all! It makes me think that I need to be careful and mindful to balance all my other responsibilities with my responsibility to him.*

This technique can be used powerfully in any gear, but it's required to fulfill the purpose of fourth gear. The point of fourth gear is to capture your exact words for your goal, and here's an example of how it's done.

And here's another scenario demonstrating how I'd use echoing, but in this case it's used to help the client give their destination a name.

Coach: *Out of all the topics we just discussed, which one stands out as most important to you?*

Client: *I don't know what to work on out of all of those things that I just talked through, but I'm unhappy about that work situation, my relationship needs help, and my income goal is very important but I also think that if I hit that income goal then I'll be much better off with everything else.*

Coach: *"If I hit that income goal." Can you tell me more about that?*

Client: *Yeah, if I can increase it by three grand a month, I'll be quite happy.*

Coach: *"Increase it by three grand a month."*

(silence)

Client: *Hm. Yeah, that's what I need to zero in on right now.*

Coach: *How much would that impact the rest of your life?*

Client: *It would make the other problems less significant, cause it would reduce my stress at the office and in my relationship. Yeah, three grand more a month.*

Coach: *Ok, "three grand more a month." If we gave your long-term goal a name or title, how well would that fit?*

Client: *Three grand more a month - yes, perfect.*

Decision Alignment

When you feel stuck in a decision-making process, I help you choose the option that aligns most closely with your internal motivations and genuine values, or to say it briefly, "what aligns better with your motivators."

The process of aligning your decisions with your motivators not only helps relieve feelings of being overwhelmed but it reminds you of what gets you out of bed in the morning. We often feel like we're "waking up in someone else's life" because we neglect to make decisions that are genuine and unique to us.

Decision alignment can be as simple as reviewing your options and asking how well each option aligns with your motivators.

Scenario demonstrating decision alignment

Client: *I feel so stressed. I have to decide whether or not to renew the lease on my apartment. I have so many things in life pending and don't feel ready for signing a 12-month lease, but it's such a great place and I love it so much. It's the perfect price and it fits my financial goals. But I can't put up with this long commute to work for another 12 months! And what if I get a contract in another state? Then I have the hassle and legal obligation of this lease.*

Coach: *Out of all options, which one best aligns with your motivator?*

Client: *Hmm. My top motivator is Freedom. The thing that would give me the most freedom overall would probably be to make sure I'm not locked into something that I am not sure about. So, ideally, I wouldn't sign another lease until I hear back about that out-of-state contract. Maybe my landlord will negotiate something shorter term with me. She is a friendly lady. Maybe she will understand. Yeah, I can maybe ask for a 6 month lease or even ask for another few weeks to make the decision.*

Coach: *Based on that, what would you like to do next?*

Client: *What I need to do between now and our next coaching conversation is negotiate something shorter term. That's my next step.*

COACHING QUESTIONS

It's time for some questions that help us name your short-term or long-term goals.

- If you could put it in just a couple of words, how would you say it?
- I heard a few ways that you phrased it. Which phrasing sounds best to you?
- If we could give your goal a movie title, what would you name it?
- The key phrase I'm hearing you say is "[insert the client's phrase]." How well does that describe your goal?
- If you could give it a name like a book title, what title would you give it?
- If you could name it like a town or a street sign, what name would you give it?

ICF CORE COMPETENCIES

As I shift into fourth gear, the final gear aimed solely at gaining clarity, I use the following ICF Core Competencies:

- Establishing the Coaching Agreement
- Active Listening

Establishing the Coaching Agreement

When I repeat your goal to you in fourth gear, we are coming to an understanding and agreement as to what goal you currently want to achieve in our coaching relationship.

A written coaching contract confirms the overall agreement between us for all conversations; however, in fourth gear, when we talk about your long-term and short-term goals, we are verbally establishing the "coaching agreement in each and every session that is specific to that session."

There is an overall written or signed coaching agreement, and then there is the verbal agreement within each live coaching conversation.

Active Listening

A coach "mirrors back what the client has said to ensure clarity and understanding." In this gear, I am asking you for the exact language you prefer for your goal, not my words. Your words will be what I write down and what we use to hold you accountable to your goal.

Exercise (Chapter 12)

In your diary, write today's date and "Chapter 12" on top of the page.

EARN 1 POINT

1. What is your current destination (long-term goal) that you're working toward? List three fun *or* practical names that you could give it. Consider a title that sounds like a movie, a book, a street sign, or a town.

EARN 1 POINT

2. What is your current next stop (short-term goal)? List three fun *or* practical names that you could give it. Consider a title that sounds like a movie, a book, a street sign, or a town.

EARN 1 POINT

3. Think of any upcoming decision you have to make - big or small. To practice "Decision Alignment," answer this question: how you can choose or decide in a way that aligns closely with your motivator? Think creatively of your options, and write down your thoughts.

MAXIMUM POINTS EARNED FOR THIS CHAPTER

You earn 1 point for completing each of the 3 questions above for a maximum of 3 points.

Count the number of points you completed and write down the total number on your Scoreboard, as described in Exercise Chapter 1.

CHAPTER 13, FIFTH GEAR - MOTIVATED ACTION

DEFINITION

First to fourth gears were about progressively gaining clarity on what's meaningful and important to you. Now, in fifth gear, I help you find a motivated and committed *next step of action to* achieve that thing which is meaningful and important to you.

At this point in the conversation, you know what you want, you feel great about it, you named it, and now, it's simply a matter of identifying your very next step and putting it on your calendar.

In a destination conversation, general examples of a next step might be designing a vision statement, creating some form of a vision board, designing a timeline or milestones for your long-term goal, establishing a new connection with someone or a group, or searching for a new kind of resource to help you get more clarity about your long-term goal.

In a next stop conversation, general examples of a next step may be more specific and direct, such as showing up to an event, applying for something, producing a special document, asking someone a question, following up on a backlog of to-do's, meeting with someone or trying to reach someone, or any other measurable and exciting actions that move you closer to your goal.

Whether it's a destination conversation or next stop conversation, the dreams that you have been talking about become real in fifth gear. That's because a dream is not a goal until it has a place on your calendar.

Dreams remain only dreams until you act on them. And to act on them, you start by thinking about your next step.

Action planning is the point of fifth gear, but not just *any kind* of action-planning. It's got to be something you *feel genuinely committed to and excited about*; otherwise, you're unlikely to have enough momentum to complete it. But don't worry, I designed a special process for making sure you plan your action with strong momentum.

CHECKLIST

The fifth gear checklist is the same for both the destination and next stop conversations.

In fifth gear, there are eight checkboxes that I tick, representing eight ways to make sure that your next step of action has the most amount of momentum behind it.

So, what are the eight boxes to tick? Here, in fifth gear, I will use what I coined the "baiting process" (the 8-point checklist below) to plan your next step of action for you to take within the next seven days or between today's coaching conversation and the next one, whichever happens first.

In third gear, you zeroed in on a long-term goal (in a destination conversation) or a short-term goal (in a next stop conversation). In fourth gear, you gave your goal a name or title. Now in fifth gear, it's time to make it happen.

I call this process baiting, not because I know much about the sport of fishing (because I don't), but rather because there are eight steps and they all start with the letter "b." If you put the letter "b" and the number "8" together, like "b-8," and say it out loud, it sounds like "bait."

From what I do know about the sport of fishing, choosing the right bait is key to landing a great catch. It's the same in coaching. Getting the right results depends on the baiting process. When done right, it will "hook" you into your goal.

In this chapter, I'll explain what each of these tick boxes mean, but you'll see there are eight of them and they all have the letter "B."

- ☑ The Bang
- ☑ The Baby Step
- ☑ The Backlog
- ☑ The Booking
- ☑ The Banking
- ☑ The Battle
- ☑ The Belief
- ☑ The Backbone

By the time we get to fifth gear, you may have already volunteered some of the items in the eight checkboxes without me even asking. If so, I might make sure I heard you correctly or that you haven't changed your mind since.

As a side note, in the Checklists chapter toward the end of this book, you'll also see a ninth checkbox in fifth gear for allowing silent processing. That is not a formal part of the baiting process; rather, it is only there as a reminder to allow for silent pauses in *every* gear, to give you space to think and process.

WHAT KIND OF ACTION DO WE DESIGN?

That next step of action that you plan for in fifth gear must be something - anything - that moves you closer to your long-term goal and that you feel compelled to do. It must be something that you *genuinely* desire doing, and you feel great about it.

However, when you're unsure about what to do next, I might offer you a challenge or an exercise to do as "homework" that I pull from my mental library of coaching tools.

I will only suggest a challenge or exercise if you seem uncertain or if you need a little boost to get your energy up and running in a more creative way.

For example, if you sound like you're struggling to find motivation for a fitness goal, I might challenge you to create some form of a visual or vision board so you can imagine yourself completing it, or maybe check out a supportive community who shares a similar goal.

As another example, if you're facing a creative block in your work, I might challenge you to a written role-playing exercise to break out of your perceived limitation. A challenge may even be more direct, like brainstorming new environments or engaging in a completely different activity to spark inspiration.

WHAT ARE THE EIGHT STEPS?

In the action-creation process, each of the eight steps start with the letter "B."

Step 1. The Bang

Many years back, the word "bang" was another word for an exclamation point "!". An exclamation point communicates strong emotion or emphasis. It often signifies substantial desire or enthusiasm.

When planning your next step, step 1 is called "the bang" because, in this step, we look for how much desire or enthusiasm you feel about reaching your goal. Whichever goal you're currently working towards, it's going to need the energy and motivation to fuel the effort that it will take to achieve it.

In this step, we make sure your goals have enough "bang" to keep you going. If we discover here that either your long-term or short-term goals need some tweaking or adjustment to make it more motivating, then we do it here.

In this step, to figure out how much "bang" you might have for your goal, I typically ask a scaling question. It can be worded in a few ways, but here's one. I ask: *How do you feel about reaching your goal, on a scale from 1 to 10? A score of "1" means you "feel no energy" and score of "10" means you "feel incredibly energized."*

If you score a 7 or below, I help you figure out how to increase the *bang* you feel for that goal. As your coach, I may ask, "How could you adjust your goal to make it more compelling for you?"

When you score an 8 or above, we continue to step 2.

Step 2. The Baby Step

Rome wasn't built in a day, and we humans are not born knowing how to file our taxes. Rather, we build and learn great things one very small step at a time. Likewise, your destination won't be fully realized the moment that you come up with it. Instead, it's going to be achieved through a number of smaller steps.

You complete a number of small actions on your way to a full-grown destination.

To keep your motivation up, it's essential your next step is small enough that it can be completed within seven days, and exciting enough that you genuinely desire accomplishing it.

At this point in the conversation, we break down how you can complete your next step - aka your *next stop* - so that it seems attainable over the next seven days or between now and our next conversation.

Step 3. The Backlog

When you think of your destination or next stop, a whole bunch of other steps may pop into your mind that you think you "need to do." Then, the more you think, the longer the list grows, and the more things that are added, your mind becomes perhaps a bit too full.

That's where the "backlog" comes in. When you think of a list of things you "need to do" to reach your destination, write them down in a backlog. Put them down in a list - not a paragraph - so that you can easily check each one off in future conversations.

Whenever you go through the baiting process, you can revisit this list to see if or how it inspires your future next steps. Of course, you can also add to or delete from this list whenever necessary.

Step 4. The Booking

The next step I take in the baiting process is to help you put your next stop on your calendar.

All sorts of industries and systems throughout the world require a booking, and your next stop is no different. When you want to go on holiday, you make a booking. Your holiday would not happen without someone booking it in and putting it onto a calendar of some sort.

When it comes to making your goals happen, if it doesn't have a place on your calendar, then it's still only a dream and not yet a goal. A goal has a clear and measurable target. The amazing thing about personal coaching is it walks you through the process of turning your dreams into goals, and then your goals into achievements.

So, how do you complete a "booking" for your next stop? Think carefully about what you might need to do for your next stop, then estimate the very least amount of time (minutes, hours, or days) that it will take. Then, estimate the very most amount of time (minutes, hours, or days) it will take.

After you identified the least amount of time and the most, calculate and write down the *middle or average of the two numbers*. For example, if it could take at least one hour and at the very most five hours, then plan to book in at least three hours.

To find the average of one hour and five hours, of course, you add the two values together and then divide by two.

Once you've found that average number, you look at your calendar and make space to fit in that time. You could book it all in one sitting or split it up into small windows of time that better fits your schedule.

For example, you might fit three hours in on Wednesday evening or you can split it into three separate one-hour sessions on Monday, Wednesday, and Thursday mornings.

It's important that you book your next stop within one week of our conversation, in order to keep your momentum and motivation up.

Note: If you cannot imagine how many hours it could take, that may be a sign to break down your next stop into smaller steps that you can estimate.

Step 5. The Banking

Banks are places where we store things of great value, such as precious items in a safe deposit box or money in a bank account. It may or may not be money and it may not be a physical object at all, but when it comes to your next stop, what is the thing or act of value that you're looking to achieve?

Is it a reply from someone? Is it a document of some sort? Is it the completion of a particular physical activity? Is it the completion of a specific transaction?

The Banking refers to anything that can serve as evidence that you completed your next stop.

We're looking for something measurable. Here are some examples:

- A person says something to confirm it's completed.
- You deliver a message to someone.

- You changed the state of something that was in a different state before you started.
- You have new knowledge that you did not have before starting.
- A clock or time-device confirmed you spent the time that you planned.
- You received a receipt, document, or a certificate.
- You can point to an observable or physical change in your body.
- You received an email that contains information you looked for.
- You received information that you asked for or looked for.
- You received money or something else valuable.

Step 6. The Battle

Have you noticed that, in all of human history, the greatest stories of achievement also include some of the greatest obstacles?

Whether it's something minor or major, you're also likely to meet with some degree of obstacles on your way to achieving your next stop. Your challenges may be emotional, mental, physical, financial, or some other form of difficulty.

This step is about preparation. An army general has a carefully strategized plan before marching into battle. He also makes sure all troops are ready; he studies enemy information and makes sure supplies can get through for his troops, among other things.

However, even before he even plans all of that, a general must first identify the opponent. In this step, we're going to identify what, if any, kinds of opponents stand between you and your next stop - small or large. Once we know what's possibly in the way, we'll strategize ways to prepare ahead of time to give you the best winning chances.

You can "prepare for battle" with only a paper and pen, or a digital notepad of some sort. I'd ask you to simply draw or insert two columns onto a page. In the first column, you write the heading "The Opponent," and in the second column write the heading "The Strategy."

The point of this exercise is to help you either prevent the opponent from rising up or lessen its overall impact on you.

Your "opponent" can be anything that opposes your progress - an emotion, an object, a lack of knowledge, a person's opinion, or anything of any kind that is likely to get in your way.

As a few random or general examples, "The Opponent" column might include:

- Feeling too tired
- No one is available to help me
- Not believing in myself
- I don't have enough information
- Jane says no

In your second column, which you titled "The Strategy," you would then counter each of the opponents with a plan of some kind, such as:

- Get 9 hours sleep the night before and/or have an extra energy drink
- Ask a friend ahead of time if they are willing to be on call if I need help
- Pick any one of several personal coaching techniques and use it, such as fast forwarding, to have a higher chance of believing in yourself
- I only need to know one thing right now to move forward so find that out first

- Prepare to thank Jane even if she says no and ask her for help on what it will take to get a yes

Step 7. The Belief

When you fully believe that you can do something, it can feel like you have already done half the work. So, in this step, we check to see how much you believe in your next stop.

On a scale of 1 to 10, with 1 meaning you don't believe and 10 meaning you completely believe, how much do you believe that you'll complete your next stop?

If you scored an 8 or above, we move on to the next step.

However, if you scored a 7 or below, we would go back to step 1 (The Bang) and work through the baiting process again to identify what needs to change so that you score an 8 or above in believing you can complete the next stop.

Step 8. The Backbone

Your physical backbone keeps you upright. It supports movement for your entire body.

Your spine or backbone is a great metaphor for this step because this is when we make sure you have the right amount of support and accountability in place to keep you moving toward your goal.

Support and accountability can look like very different to each person. It could be a reminder on your phone to check in with yourself and your progress, a motivational note taped to your mirror, or a person who has agreed to help you in some way.

The simplicity or complexity of the support you need depends on you and the nature of your next stop. You might need a simple note with your favorite quote on it or a detailed checklist that includes a call with a friend or your coach.

In this step, you answer my question, "What kind of additional support or accountability, if any, will you put in place to ensure you complete this next stop?

And that completes the baiting process. By the end, you're hooked into your next step.

TECHNIQUES AND TOOLS

Measurable Goals

It's kind of hard to celebrate a goal if you're unsure whether or not you achieved it. That's one of the reasons why it's important that goals be *measurable* - so that you know when you've achieved it.

Whether it's your next stop or your destination, it's my job to help you make goals measurable. Measurable goals are the kind that you can point to or count in some way. That might mean pointing to the clock to say you invested the time that you intended, or it might mean pointing to a certain document, or pointing to something a person does, or something else. Maybe it's an email that someone sent. Maybe it's the completion of a new form of physical exercise that you wanted to try, or maybe even it's the new personal trainer you hired.

If you can point to it or count it, it's measurable.

In the baiting process, Step 5, The Banking, we're looking for that measurable thing - something you can point to or count - which points to you completing your next stop.

Vision Board or Action Board

The brain is wired for reward.

Reward might even be critical to survival. In one study, researchers removed the reward-chemical (dopamine) from mice. And the result? The mice stopped eating altogether and died.[17]

On a neurological and biological level, reward appears to be your key to action and life. You must clearly feel and envision a reward, or else you'll likely have a difficult time persevering.

In a coaching conversation, to help you stay mindful of your reward, I might propose the challenge of creating any form of a vision board that can be placed somewhere you look every day, such as on a refrigerator, your phone's wallpaper, a desk at work, a bathroom mirror, the dashboard of your car, or on top of a bed stand.

Neuroscientist Dr. Tara Swart refers to vision boards as "action boards," because visualizing your goal allows your brain to start coming up with actionable steps.

No matter what you call it, a vision board has any number of images, words, or a collage of images and words that you make from your own digital or physical clippings. It can also be something you draw, paint, or write out in words. Each word or visual represents something that lights you up inside and reminds you of where you're headed.

It helps to give you a sense of purpose, and the repetitive action of imagining the achieving of those goals can significantly reduce fear or stress.

Multibillion-dollar companies document their visions and share them with the world, and business consultants incorporate vision board workshops as part of employee development programs. Documenting a vision is a powerful tool.

Whether it's only words on a page or only imagery or a combination of both, a vision board helps you keep your eyes on the reward you're currently working toward.

Sometimes a vision board is simply a piece of paper on which you've written out your vision in detail in the form of a several-paragraph essay. Other times, it's only pictures. If I am trying to get physically fit, I may have a vision board that has pictures of me at a time when I was fit.

Sometimes, the image or words represent exactly what you're trying to achieve. Other times, the images or words might be very general and serve as a kind of breadcrumb to getting better clarity on your goals.

If it triggers a sense of a reward for you, then it belongs on the vision board.

Visual or Audible Reminders

Writing out your next stop and putting it somewhere you can see it *can help you get it done*. Research published by Dominican University stated that writing goals down contributed to a 42% increase in achievement.[18]

Writing it down - either digitally or physically - will help. With many thousands of your internal thoughts plus external events and people all competing for your attention throughout the day and week, it might be very easy to forget exactly what next step you committed to with your coach.

However, by setting visual or audible reminders, you give yourself a better chance of actually remembering and completing your short-term goal.

A visual reminder can be anything at all that you place somewhere clearly visible, such as your bathroom mirror or setting a pop up reminder on a digital task list that you use regularly.

An audible reminder can be anything from an alarm to a friendly reminder phone call from someone.

My personal favorite reminders are my smart phone calendar, alarm clock, sticky notes, and my magnetic whiteboard on the fridge.

Scaling Questions

Scaling questions are used in multiple professional contexts, including the medical world. When it comes to professional coaching, scaling questions are used most often to measure your level of motivation, satisfaction, or interest. A scaling question I might ask is, "On a scale of 1 to 10, with 10 meaning it couldn't get any better and 1 meaning it couldn't get any worse, how do you feel about [insert your goal]?"

If the answer is 7, I'll ask, "What would it take to bump it up to an 8 or 9?"

If the score is 6 or lower, then your motivation is too low. Any score of 6 or below means it is time to shift into reverse gear and come up with a new plan.

When a score is an 8 or above in motivation, satisfaction, or interest, then it's generally healthy to move forward. Otherwise, the topic needs adjusting, redefining, or changing in some way. Most of the time, a score of 7 or below will simply not have enough energy behind it.

Scaling questions are essential when deciding on your long-term goal or destination, so that we know how much fuel you have in you.

Scenario to demonstrate scaling questions

Coach: *On a scale of 1 to 10, 1 being you couldn't be any less motivated, and 10 being you couldn't be any more motivated, how motivated are you to complete this goal?*

Client: *About a 7.*

Coach: *What, if anything, in the world would bump that up to an 8 or 9?*

Client: *I guess if I had my brother's support, that would help.*

Coach: *What comes to mind when you consider asking your brother for support?*

Client: *He totally would. I simply have to ask him. I just didn't think of it until you asked but, yeah, that will bump my motivation to an 8 or more.*

COACHING QUESTIONS

Questions to Establish "The Bang"

- On a scale of 1-10, with "10" meaning the *most motivated* and "1" meaning *the least*, how motivated do you feel to complete this?
- How well does this action align with your motivators?
- What could you change about this goal that will make it more meaningful or fulfilling?
- What could you change about this goal that will make it more fun or exciting?

Questions to Identify "The Baby Step"

- What is the very next step for you to make it happen?
- What's your first or next step?
- Where would you like to start?

- What is the first thing you need to do to get started?
- What's the most you can imagine doing over the next seven days, and what's the minimum?
- What could you do to start mapping that out?
- In the perfect world with no limits on you, how would you make it happen?
- What can you do this week to get closer to your goal?
- How could you break this down into smaller, more manageable steps?
- What step would you like to take between now and the next time we speak?
- Imagine it's seven days from now and you've very happily completed your next step. What next step could that be?
- What's the next step you could take to get you closer to your vision?
- What choices do you have?
- What needs to happen for ___ to be true?
- If you could make ___ happen, how would you do it?
- What research could you do to help you find the first or next step?
- What information would you need to find the answer?
- What kind of research might help you find the answer?

Questions to Set Up "The Backlog"

- Where would you like to keep your list of "to do" items for this long-term goal?
- Out of all your options for your next step, which ones can go into your backlog?
- I hear several things that you would like to do. How much would it help you to add them to a backlog?
- How many of those things would you like to keep in a to-do list for next week?

Questions to Make "The Booking"

- What's the least amount of time it could take and what's the most?
- What's the shortest time it could take to complete this?
- What's the longest time it could take to complete this?
- What's a healthy middle ground between longest and shortest time?
- What days or times would you like to do this?
- What is the time and date you'd like to complete this step and what is a backup day and time if the first one doesn't work out?
- How useful would it be to look at your calendar and pick out a time and a backup time?
- By what date or dates will you complete this action?
- Ok, those are your target dates. Now, what are your backup dates?
- What will you do to work this into your schedule this week?

Questions to Identify "The Banking"

- How will you know when you have fulfilled this goal?
- What signs will there be when you have achieved this goal?
- What evidence will there be to prove to yourself that you've completed this action?
- Who, if anyone, will notice when you complete this action?

- How will you know that you have achieved or reached this goal?
- Your next step is to spend time this week on your goal. How will you know that you have spent enough time?
- What will be the proof that you've completed this goal?

Questions to Prepare for "The Battle"

- What external opposition might get in the way of you accomplishing this action?
- What internal opposition might get in the way of you accomplishing this action?
- How can you prepare yourself for each obstacle ahead of time?
- What kind of thoughts will you need to have daily to overcome this?

Questions to Establish "The Belief"

- How believable is it that you can complete this step by the date you set?
- Taking into consideration all the other commitments you have this week, how confident are you that you will achieve this goal?
- On a scale of 1 to 10, how believable is this next step?
- How ready do you feel to do what it takes to get there?

Questions to Build "The Backbone"

- How can you remind yourself to take this action?
- How, if at all, would you like me to encourage you between now and our next session?
- What support do you need to ensure it gets done?
- What can you do to get that support?
- Why is it important to get support to make it happen?
- What kind of environment or setting would help the most?
- Who can you ask?
- Who else, if anyone, can you ask?
- Who are some people who might be able to offer more information?
- When would you like to have our next coaching conversation?
- When would you like to talk next?

ICF CORE COMPETENCIES

In fifth gear, I'm primarily using the following ICF Core Competencies:
- Designing Actions
- Planning and Goal Setting
- Managing Progress and Accountability

Designing Actions

As we enter this gear, we "define actions that will enable [you] to demonstrate, practice, and deepen new learning." In other words, by using the baiting method, you uncover and learn the most important things you need to know to prepare yourself for your next step.

Planning and Goal Setting

As we design each action, we'll create "a plan with results that are attainable, measurable, specific, and have target dates." The fifth gear uses the name of the goal, covers its attainability, uses carefully estimated time frames, puts the goal on the calendar, and covers several more considerations that are often overlooked in a typical goal setting conversation,

Managing Progress and Accountability

A professional coach is someone who "clearly requests...actions that will move [you] toward [your] stated goals." Fifth gear's "baiting process" allows me covers eight areas that move you toward your goals.

Exercise (Chapter 13)

In your diary, write today's date and "Chapter 13" on top of the page.

EARN 1 POINT

1. This week, there might be several options for actions that you can take to move closer toward your destination (long-term goal). What are two or three actions you can take?

Write down a short brainstorm of two or three potential actions. Each one can be either big or small actions but all must be doable within one week from today.

EARN 1 POINT

2. Pick your favorite option from your list above, and circle it.

EARN UP TO 8 POINTS

3. Now, using the one action that you circled in number 2 above, run through all eight steps of the baiting process to earn this third point.

In your diary, write down the name of each of the eight steps and, next to each, write down your response to each one.

By the end of the eight steps, you will have a next step of action that you can take this week.

MAXIMUM POINTS EARNED FOR THIS CHAPTER

You earn 1 point each for completing the first and second question, and you earn up to 8 points for completing the third question, for a maximum of 10 points.

Count the number of points you completed and write down the total number on your Scoreboard, as described in Exercise Chapter 1.

CHAPTER 14, NEUTRAL GEAR - CHECK IN

DEFINITION

Neutral gear is when I take a moment to pause the conversation and check in on how you're feeling about where it's headed.

It's like zooming out to consider the topic we're discussing and how you feel about it, in order to evaluate whether or not you want to take a different or new direction.

I can stop and shift into neutral gear at any point in the conversation, but it normally happens anytime between third and fifth gear.

I can use any number of questions to "shift" into this gear, but a basic and direct one is, "I normally take a moment to make sure you're happy with the direction of the conversation. So, how do you feel about the direction of the conversation at this point?" or "Are you getting what you need from this coaching conversation right now?"

Depending on your answer, I might shift down or up a gear.

For example, if we are in third gear and then I shift into neutral, I may discover that there's a lot on your mind that you need to talk about. In that case, we might shift back into second gear for a braindump to help you think out loud and put your thoughts in order.

Or as another example, if we're in fourth gear, and I shift into neutral to ask how you're going with the conversation, I may discover that we need to shift down into third gear to get more clarity about your goal, then return back to fourth gear only after you have achieved clarity.

CHECKLIST

- ☑ Check if you are ready to shift up a gear (tachometer)
- ☑ Check which gear we need to shift down to, if needed (tachometer)
- ☑ Allow silent pauses for processing

TECHNIQUES AND TOOLS

The Tachometer

The tachometer is a physical instrument in a car that displays a number, and that number represents how fast the engine is turning, aka the RPM or Revolutions Per Minute. In a manual car (also referred to as a "stick shift"), the tachometer lets you know when it's the best time to shift gears for the sake of the engine's health.

In coaching, a tachometer is a metaphor for measuring the best time to shift gears in the conversation. If it's going well, we shift up a gear. If it's not going well, we either shift down a gear or into reverse.

In a car, shifting at the wrong time can damage the transmission; it's just like a coaching conversation, where shifting too soon or too late can damage the momentum you feel. The last thing I want to do is mess with your "transmission."

The "transmission" of our conversation is equivalent to your state of motivation.

In a real car, if you switch from a low to a high gear too quickly, the car will labor with difficulty and won't accelerate properly. If you shift down a gear too quickly, it could make the entire car skid across the highway.

Just as I would frequently glance at the dashboard of my car every so often while driving, likewise I'll keep an eye on the metaphorical tachometer in our conversation as we shift through the gears.

Motivation is defined as "a desire or willingness to do something; enthusiasm."[19] The more desire you have, the greater your motivation. So, you might say that measuring your degree of motivation is comparable to the RPM of a car's transmission. Your amount of desire, enthusiasm, and willingness to move on to the next gear is your RPM.

How revved up are you to get clarity and take action? In other words, you must feel good.

Not just good, but very good.

What does it mean to feel "good?"

Feeling bad about your goal won't get you very far, but feeling good about your goal gives you power.

Since "feeling good" can often refer to things that are actually *no good* for you, I will be a bit more precise about what I mean. In context of a coaching conversation, I like to equate the phrase "feeling good" with "feeling hope."

Hopefulness appears to be the foundation of feeling good enough to reach your goals. There are researchers who believe this, too.

Charles Snyder revealed how much of an impact hope, or the lack thereof, has on our lives, and many studies have since backed up his research.[20]

Snyder found that hope improved people's performance in all kinds of activities, anywhere from racing to academic testing.

When study participants felt hopeful, they put more energy into their efforts. They showed more creativity when trying to overcome challenges. People who didn't feel hopeful did not exert themselves to achieve the goals he set for them.

When thinking that they would fail from the outset, they didn't have the motivation to try. If they did try but then became stuck, they gave up quickly. They didn't have the motivation to find different pathways to their goals.

Feeling good and feeling motivated requires hope. It's a must if you want to keep going.

The idea of the tachometer helps me remember to check for a strong sense of hope throughout the conversation.

How do I use the tachometer?

I don't move to the next gear without you feeling good.

As your coach, I listen to the way you answer a question. If you feel low on motivation or low on hope, I can ask a provocative question to "rev up the engine."

If you're not happy in a gear, then I don't move on. If you didn't give me an answer with energy, I ask questions to get the energy you need to progress to the next gear.

I listen for things you say that bring you energy.

I might catch you quickly deflate or change the subject with an unhappy tone of voice. A quick deflation is usually a sign of something getting in the way, and it needs to be addressed. There could be a huge source of motivation and energy released when we overcome a thought that was getting in the way.

I take extra time to ask questions until we come to a more deeply felt answer or a greater sense of motivation. Then, when you seem to be feeling good again, I go ahead and shift into the next gear.

Although questions are often the best way to gauge your enthusiasm, there are other methods such as making observations, acknowledgments, validations, and celebrations - all of which have the potential to bring that tachometer to the place it needs to be in order to shift up a gear.

Reset Button

Most people have at least one reset button. Your reset button is that thing (or a few things) that you do which makes you feel mentally or emotionally refreshed again. It's whatever action you take that reboots your metaphorical computer, clearing the bugs that made it run slow.

It may be a 5-minute meditation, a good night's sleep, a power nap, a drive out on the highway with the windows down, a coffee, a fresh sweet mandarin, listening to a certain genre of music, dancing, or maybe a hug. One person's reset buttons may look radically different than the next person's.

Your reset button regulates you and brings you back into focus. As your coach, it's important for me to discover your unique reset buttons so I can remind you of them when needed.

I'm a coach, but I also have a coach, and she knows my reset buttons. She knows the handful of things that consistently get me feeling mentally refreshed. A gym session, a particular podcast, and a little dance lesson session are just a few of mine.

One good way to discover your reset buttons is to look at your patterns in the past to see what's worked for you. As a coach, I might simply ask you, "What have you done in the past to feel reset or refreshed?" They can be very small or simple acts, like turning on a song, or they can be longer and more complex like joining a local fitness competition.

The shorter time that it takes for your reset button, the better! That's because the quicker it is, the more frequently and easily you can reset. It's easier for most people to turn on an amazing song for two minutes to reset, rather than to plan and prepare for a marathon. Both are good, but the more quick and simple ones you can think of, the better.

Scenario demonstrating how to use the reset button

Client: *I feel like crap today.*

Coach: *What have you done in the past to make yourself feel better?*

Client: *To feel better in the past, I tend to just write everything down in a list to clear my mind and listen to some music. Yeah, maybe I'll take a minute to do that.*

(Then, in a coaching conversation on a later date...)

Client: *I'm a bit down right now. Everything just feels so blah.*

Coach: *How do you feel if I make an observation?*

Client: *Sure, that's fine.*

Coach: *I remember that when you write everything down in a list, it clears your mind. Also, listening to some music.*

Client: *Oh, yeah. Right. Well... yeah, if I do that today, I'd probably feel a bit better.*

Coach: *How helpful or unhelpful would that be to spend a few minutes on that right now during this conversation?*

Client: *Hah, yeah ok. Yeah, that will help. I'll get a pen and paper for a list.*

Gratitude Challenge

When you need to get out of an emotional funk, a gratitude challenge can have powerful transformational effects, whether it's a gratitude list, gratitude journal, verbal affirmation of gratitude, or any one of many potential gratitude exercises.

One of the quickest and easiest gratitude challenges is to stop and write down a list of things you're grateful for right now - this moment, and the key is to think of even the smallest things.

Scenario demonstrating a gratitude challenge

Client: *I feel like hell. Nothing's going right with my goals.*

Coach: *How much interest do you have in a gratitude challenge right now?*

Client: *I honestly don't know if I can do it, but I'll try.*

Coach: *Okay, what's one tiny thing you can find to be grateful for in this situation?*

Client: *Well, at least the weather was lovely today. It's boring but true.*

Coach: *Okay, we have one. What's a second?*

Client: *Well, I saw a unique-looking butterfly. It did make me smile. I forgot about that because I had to run to a meeting. The butterfly did give me a strange sense of inspiration.*

Coach: *That's two. What about a third?*

Client: *Actually, thinking of that butterfly reminds me of an inspirational graphic that I have saved on my photo gallery. It's about my power of choice in life, my power to change. Is that gratitude though? Yeah, it is, cause it makes me feel grateful. Hold on let me get that so I can tell it to you.*

(Client reads the graphic)

Coach: *How do you feel right now looking at the graphic?*

Client: *Hah, well, better than a few moments ago. That gratitude trick got me out of my funk.*

COACHING QUESTIONS

- How do you feel about the direction of this conversation so far?
- Overall, how do you feel about this conversation right now?
- I just heard excitement in your voice when you said ___. What else can you tell me about that?
- I hear a sigh. What does that sigh mean?
- I hear a change in your tone of voice. What does that mean?
- I hear a change in the pitch of your voice. What does that mean?
- I hear a change in speed in your talking. What does that mean?
- How are you feeling right now?
- How do you feel about the conversation right now?
- What, if anything, could you change about this conversation to increase your energy?
- So, we've come to our 30-minute mark, and I want to check in. What are you feeling right now?
- How well are we doing with getting what you need from this conversation?
- How satisfied are you with your progress so far?
- How energized do you feel by that?
- What, if anything, might make this conversation better for you?
- If you could, how would you make it more fun?

- How are we doing in achieving your goal?
- Are you getting what you need right now in this conversation?
- In light of your goal and the fact that we have ___ minutes left, how do you feel about where we are in this conversation?

ICF CORE COMPETENCIES

The two most important Core Competencies for this gear are:
- Active Listening
- Coaching Presence

Active Listening

When you gain or lose a sense of hope, your "concerns, goals, values and beliefs about what is and is not possible" also changes.

In neutral gear, I'm sensitive to and listening for your sense of hope, enthusiasm, and motivation. It does not make sense to move onto the next gear unless you feel energized about the direction we're headed.

Coaching Presence

The questions I ask in neutral gear allow for a conversation style that is "open, flexible and confident." Coaching presence requires the flexibility to shift up or down a gear, openness to change direction at any time, and confidence as to which direction to go.

Exercise (Chapter 14)

In your diary, write today's date and "Chapter 14" on top of the page.

EARN 1 POINT

1. To earn this point, think about the past 24 hours. Over that time, what are at least five things that you can feel grateful for? They can be very big or very little things. You might feel a large amount of gratitude, or you might feel the tiniest amount of gratitude, and both count. Your list of things can be anything at all - no limits.

Write five of them down. That is your gratitude challenge.

EARN 1 POINT

2. What are some of your healthy reset buttons that you either currently use or that you've used in the past? In other words, think about anytime in your life, past or present, when you have taken action to make yourself feel reset or refreshed emotionally or mentally.

The more simple the action, the better.

These are your reset buttons.

EARN 1 POINT

3. How do you feel about the questions you've answered in this Chapter 14 exercise? Right now, take 20 or 30 seconds to check in how you feel about what you've written, and then write down at least one sentence.

This is like checking your "tachometer," as introduced earlier in this chapter.

MAXIMUM POINTS EARNED FOR THIS CHAPTER

You earn 1 point for completing each of the 3 questions above for a maximum of 3 points.

Count the number of points you completed and write down the total number on your Scoreboard, as described in Exercise Chapter 1.

CHAPTER 15, REVERSE GEAR - OVERCOME OBSTACLES

DEFINITION

At any point in a coaching conversation, you may hit an obstacle which threatens to "pop the tire" of your progress, motivation, or clarity. As your coach, it's my job to recognize it and then shift into reverse gear in those moments.

At any point between second and fifth gear, I might shift into reverse gear to ask questions that help you "back out" of a restrictive, immobilizing, or obstructive way of thinking. In other words, I ask questions that get you moving forward again, so that we can progress through all gears.

REVERSE GEAR CHECKLIST

☑ Identify and challenge disabling beliefs.

☑ Convert "I don't want" to "what I do want."

☑ Allow silent pauses for processing

TECHNIQUES AND TOOLS

Disabling Beliefs:

As a coach, it's important for me to recognize beliefs that metaphorically injure or "disable" you from moving forward (stopping progress, motivation, or clarity).

When I see that you've run into a disabling belief, I back our conversational "car" into reverse to get you out of that unhelpful head space or heart space, and then I ask questions that will help you find a (metaphorically) unobstructed road of thought.

Disabling beliefs come in three major forms:

- Self-distorting beliefs called "monsters"
- Blanket statements
- Translations

Those three disabling beliefs can show up in any gear of a coaching conversation. Sometimes they come up a couple times over an hour, and other times a client seems so flooded with disabling beliefs that we only have time to address the biggest ones.

We humans tend to think negative thoughts fairly often.

Psychiatrist and author, Dr. Dennis Gersten, a diplomat of the American Board of Psychiatry and Neurology, said in an interview that "the average person runs about 15,000 thoughts per day in which at least half of those are negative."[21]

While studies vary on how many thoughts the average human has per day - whether it's 6,000, 15,000, or more - the fact that half of them can be negative means that, as your coach, I have a lot of work to do as I help you steer clear toward your goals.

In the next few sections, I'll introduce the three major types of "disabling beliefs" that tend to get in your way during a coaching conversation.

Monster

Your monster is that little voice inside of your head that distorts your perception of yourself, making you believe that you're not good enough in some way.

Distortion is the key word here. The key visual difference between humans and monsters is grossly distorted body parts like abnormally large mouths filled with sharp teeth, excessively wide torso or limbs, or other disproportionate facial features.

In coaching, a monster represents a distortion of self-perception and the apprehension that follows that distortion. So, a monster is a coaching term that symbolizes your distorted beliefs about yourself and the fear or apprehension that follows those beliefs.

To weaken the power of the monster and address its alteration of the truth, the first step is to name the monster. By giving the monster a name, you can begin to address it directly and remove a significant degree of its intimidating power.

Whether you give it a serious name or a funny one, after naming the monster, we can then use imagination to further weaken the monster's power.

For example, you may fear changing your career because of your monster saying, "I'm not young enough" or you may be apprehensive about starting a fitness pursuit because, "My body isn't strong enough to handle the gym."

In a coaching conversation, I might ask you, "What can you name the voice that is telling you that you are not young enough?" or "What can you name the voice that is telling you that your body isn't strong enough?"

In those cases, maybe you'll come up with names for your monster like "The Agist," "The Liar," or a funny name like "Sparkles."

If it's appropriate in the moment, making it a funny name can remove even more of its power of intimidation."

After you name your monster, then I may ask, "If you could explain to [insert monster's name] at least one small way in which their statement could possibly be incorrect, what would you say?"

Another way might be, "If it were possible that you could help [insert monster's name] to believe in you just a little more, what would you say to it?"

But the best question might be, "What evidence in the world contradicts this belief?"

To this day, I know my own monster, and it's the same as it was over ten years ago when I first recognized it with my coach and gave it a name. Because it now has a name, I can quickly recognize that form of disabling belief rather than mindlessly obey it out of fear, confusion, or anxiety. It's like recognizing that I have dirt on my clothes and then wiping it off.

Blanket Statements

A blanket statement is any idea or belief that *feels smothering to your potential* and which you assume *will always be true* about life, yourself, others, or the world.

Blanket statement beliefs throw everything under a blanket without exception.

Blanket statements typically use the words "all," "they all," "every," "always," "never," "all the time," or "every time."

Yes, it might be true many events are highly likely to happen due to probability and statistics, but nothing is "always" the case, specifically when it comes to your potential.

"Always" and any word that means the same, has no secure basis in our physical world. Everything at a molecular level is constantly changing. The continuous movement, reactions, and transformations at a molecular level introduce variability and exceptions to every rule or statement about the physical universe.

Nothing in the material, tangible universe remains the same - not even laws of physics. Fundamental laws of physics, like Newton's laws, have exceptions at quantum levels, demonstrating that there are almost always nuances and exceptions to every rule.

When it comes to coaching, we are only concerned with blanket statements that feel like a smothering blanket is being thrown over your *potential*.

An example of a blanket statement thought might be, "I really want to tell her but she has never listened in the past, so she won't listen today if I share this new idea,"

As a coach, it is my job to help you probe these thoughts, and it could be as simple as asking, "How true is that?" or, "What would happen if this time it was different?"

Another example of a blanket statement might be, "I'm very excited about this idea, but my client will hate this change in our services because it's so different to what we've offered before."

As your coach who recognizes your blanket statement, I might ask, "On a scale of 1 to 10, how true is that?" or "What are some ways that you can disprove that belief?"

I remember once hating something about my job and thinking, "It would be wonderful to change this, but my boss would *never* let me do that." That was my blanket statement holding me from my potential and "never" was the word that smothered me and my potential. It was my personal coach at the time who recognized that disabling belief and challenged it by asking me, "How true is *never*?"

It was one of many of her miracle-working coaching questions that changed my career and life. After recognizing the disabling belief, I asked for what I wanted, my boss *did* let me make the major change, and to this day, I look back on that disabling belief like an old jail cell I've been freed from.

Translations

In coaching, "translations" refer to your assumptions about what a person, a group of people, or an organization means by their actions or by their words, all without direct verbal confirmation from the source. It is only a disabling belief, however, if it stops you from *taking important action* or *hinders your potential*.

When you "translate" a language, you hear the foreign word and then figure out what it means in your own language. Mistranslations happen often; they often happen even when two people speak the same language!

I once asked for a side of pickles in a restaurant, but instead of a couple large, crisp, green garlic dill pickles that I had in my mind, the waitress served me a small plate of three extremely thin, floppy, sliced cucumbers and onions. That's what the restaurant understood as "pickles."

Why don't I call these kinds of disabling beliefs "*mis*translations"? Because my goal is to find the better or more true interpretation of what the person or source said, which could be the more accurate translation.

For example, you may say, "My boss was really upset during the meeting today. I think he hated the work I did on the project." In that case, you're translating the boss' upset attitude as being related to your work, when in reality, your boss could have been upset about a bad-news phone call that he received before the meeting or some other project issue.

As your coach, I could respond by asking something along the lines of, "What is another possibility for his attitude?" or, "If you could interpret that in the best way possible, what else could that mean?"

As in the example of a "side of pickles," words can be innocently understood in a large number of ways. So can actions. I'm here to help you make sure you're not missing out on your goal, based on two different ideas of pickles.

Interrupting

Sometimes, you may need a little help refocusing on your original goal during a conversation. So, as your coach, I may interrupt you in the middle of your thought process to pause the moment and refocus the conversation on your goal.

Why should I interrupt you at all? You've paid me to be your coach, the service of keeping you accountable - getting clear and moving forward. So, I'm here to make sure you get the full value of the service you've paid for. Keeping you accountable to your goal(s) is what we agreed for services to include.

Sometimes a conversation will take a temporary new direction because something urgent has come up for you, and that's ok. However, other times, you may desperately wish to be called back to your original topic to keep you on track amidst another distracting event that's happening. So, I will interrupt to see which direction you want to go.

Scenario to demonstrate interrupting

Coach: *I'll gently interrupt here or press pause on this topic just to make sure I'm doing my job here. How do you feel about that?*

Client: *Oh. Yeah, that's fine.*

Coach: *Your goal for this conversation is to find a way to de-stress before your next presentation. We are now discussing your dog's next visit to the vet. How do these two topics weigh against each other in importance to you?*

Client: *Yeah the dog thing is just another stressful topic. Ok, let's get back to destressing.... What puts my mind in de-stress mode? Hmm...*

Unstucking

Unstucking is a fun way to refer to converting your "don't want" mentality to what you "do want." If you don't convert it, you tend to remain "stuck" with what you don't want.

As your coach, I look out for your "I don't want" thought that's getting in the way of your progress, and then help you use the "don't want" in order to identify its opposite or what it is that you "do want."

I can guarantee that in every conversation, you will have some form of an "I don't want..." statement. A guarantee is a big commitment on my part, but If you didn't have these thoughts, you wouldn't necessarily need me!

Chances are that your "don't want" thoughts will dominate your thought process until you replace it with what you "do want."

If you don't want something, the feeling of repulsion stays strong in your mind. It's like skiing down a mountain thinking, "I don't want to hit a tree, I don't want to hit a tree!"

If you don't convert your focus to what you *do want*, then you will likely focus on trees and hit one of them.

The words "do not" have an unusual power. Harvard Professor and social psychologist, Dan Wegner, showed in a study that, when asked *not to think* about something, people thought about it significantly *more* than the people who were asked to think about it. This is called Ironic Process Theory.[22]

Returning to the skiing metaphor, if you recognize hitting trees as something you *don't want* and then ask yourself "What *do I want* to focus on?" Then you begin to focus your eyes on the finish line ahead of you and therefore have a much greater chance of arriving safely down the mountain.

As your coach, I help you get unstuck from what you "don't want" to what you "do want."

Listening for Contradictions

As your coach, I listen for contradictions in what you say and then ask you what they mean, so that we can create a deeper awareness of how your thoughts may be hindering or progressing you toward your goals.

I look for three kinds of contradictions:

- Your tone of voice vs. your words
- Your destination vs. current goal in discussion
- What you want vs. what you want

Your tone of voice vs. your words

The first contradiction is the difference between your tone of voice and the words you're saying. The way you speak is more important than the words you say.

Client: *I am excited.*

Coach: *May I make an observation?*

Client: *Uhm, sure*

Coach: *I heard you say you are excited while your tone of voice sounded not excited. What did that mean?*

Client: *I mean, I am excited but just not feeling great.*

Coach: *What do you mean by you're "excited but"?*

Client: *Ok, well there's one thing that's really bothering me about this, but I would be excited for real if it weren't true.*

Your destination vs. current goal in discussion

The second contradiction is the difference between the destination you decided to work toward and what may sound like a new contradictory goal you're starting to talk about. You are free to change your destination, but I hold you accountable to whichever destination you choose until you decide otherwise.

For example, your original long-term goal was to work for a brand-new company, but now you're talking about looking for a new opportunity at your current job. That sounds like a contradiction of destination: brand new company vs. new opportunity at current job.

It might turn out that you want a new role at a brand new company, and this current new job is your next step to get there. However, I check in with you and make no assumptions.

If I spot a contradiction I would say, "You have been working toward [insert your destination here], and now, we're talking about [insert new goal]. What, if anything is the relationship between the two?" or "How important is it for you to design a long term goal that allows for both possibilities?"

It's okay to change destinations or rename your destination to allow for more possibilities. At any time, we can fix any contradictions by downshifting back to a destination conversation to redesign a better goal.

What you want vs. what you want

The third contradiction is between the statements you make in the same conversation. For example, at the beginning of the session you said you want a new car, but, a few minutes later you say you want to keep your car.

I may bring this contradiction to your attention by saying, "Earlier, you said you wanted a new car, and now, you say you want to keep the car you have. What is the relationship between these two desires?" or "How important is it for you to redefine your goal to allow for greater possibilities?"

Rewinding

Rewinding is a playful exercise to help reduce or even remove embarrassment, disappointment, or shame over something you did or said, and replace it with a light-hearted confidence to do it better the next time.

After telling me something you did or said that you did not like, I ask you to retell the story with a twist: change your actions in the story to be what you wanted them to be.

It's like the coaching tool of "fast forwarding," which I introduced earlier in this book. In both rewinding and fast forwarding, you're entering a playful mode, which actually can help you develop a degree of strength and confidence.

Rewinding begins to break the shame, self-hate, and fear surrounding an event, and you can better prepare for when that situation happens in the future.

Scenario demonstrating rewinding

Client: *I would like to change the way I talk... to have a better relationship with others, and also succeed at work.*

Coach: *What do you mean by "change the way I talk?"*

Client: *I find I often say things that push people away without me meaning to. It's very important for me to communicate correctly, to choose my words carefully. Because I'm in customer service , I should never push people away. I really need to fix that.*

Coach: *What is an example of the kind of language you are using?*

Client: *I've been told that I use a lot of negative language and that I'm too direct. I don't say much, you know, but when I have something to say, I say it. Sometimes, it seems too blunt. For example, yesterday, I had a customer who was clearly lying! He was saying that he didn't know that by cancelling his contract, he would have to pay a $100 fee. I pretty much accused him of lying... It didn't go well.*

Coach: *Okay, so, what if we imagine rewinding back to that moment in time, and what if we make believe that you are back in that conversation with your client right now, and you have a chance to say and do something better or different. What would you say or do?*

Client: *Well, I would have started to tell the client that I understand his frustration and then, show him the section in his contract that states the fee. And I would finish on a positive note by offering him something for his business.*

Anchoring

Anchoring is an empowering tool. It's a physical gesture you make that instantly connects you to an emotion you'd like to feel. This instant emotion has the potential to give you the edge you need to make a better decision, act with more confidence, or turn a negative thought-path around.

If there was a moment you felt especially confident, you can anchor it and relive it when you need a boost of confidence. If there was a moment you felt particularly calm, you can anchor that and relive it when you feel stressed. If there was a moment you felt especially smart or wise, you can anchor it and relive it when you need to make a key decision. You can pick any feeling to anchor.

How do you set an anchor? You can do this with your coach or you can do it alone.

First, decide on a physical pose that you want to attach or anchor to a feeling. The pose may be as large as standing with your arms up in a victory "V" shape, or it can be as small as sitting down while pressing your middle finger and thumb together tightly.

Personally, I prefer to use the middle finger and thumb pressing against each other.

Second, get a timer (smart phones are useful for this) and set it for two minutes. During those two minutes, hold the pose or gesture firmly with your eyes closed the entire time.

Third, while holding the pose or gesture, describe a time when you felt the desired emotion or feeling. Intentionally keep returning to the memory, holding and reliving the emotion and the moment. In your mind and heart, see, feel, hear, taste, or touch as much as possible to anchor the feeling.

Sometimes, it's easier to do this with a coach who can ask you questions about the moment to help stir stronger emotion.

When the timer ends, you've set the anchor.

After that, whenever there is a time that you need a reminder, empowerment, or encouragement, hold the same position again to relive the emotion and deepen the strength of the memory.

And that's it! It sounds simple, but it might give you the emotional edge or mental strength that you need in a difficult situation, such as right before you walk into an important meeting, immediately before getting on stage, or the night before a big event.

Scenario demonstrating anchoring

Client: *I need to talk to my boss, but I'm so nervous about it.*

Coach: *When was the last time you talked to your boss feeling very confident?*

Client: *I felt very confident one day when I went in and asked for a raise because I had done the research to prove I deserved one.*

Coach: *Would you be interested in going through a technique that may help give you a boost of confidence?*

Client: *Yes, sure.*

Coach: *The technique is called anchoring. To get started, please press your middle finger and thumb together. Hold it there until I say, "Let go."*

Client: *Okay, I am doing it now.*

Coach: *Now, describe in vivid detail again that day you felt confident. Describe as many sensations and feelings as you can remember.*

Client: (holding middle finger and thumb together tightly) *I walked into my boss' office and sat down. I felt good because I was confident. I knew that I wanted a raise. I didn't hesitate and I had all the arguments.*

Coach: *What else did you feel or hear or see or touch at that moment?*

Client: *I felt the leather sofa under me. The sun was shining through the windows. I felt a calm determination in my chest. I even looked my boss straight in the eyes... I looked at him so hard, that he probably felt my look more powerfully than ever!*

Coach: *Okay, with your fingers still pressed, let's spend the next 60 seconds with you simply sitting with all those feelings and that exact scenario in your mind. For all 60 seconds, reimagine the moment and feel all the emotions from that time even more deeply. When the 60 seconds are up, I'll let you know.*

Coach: *Okay, 60 seconds have passed, you can let go. Going back to where we were before this exercise, you were feeling nervous about talking to your boss. Now, place your fingers together again as you did in our anchoring exercise and answer this question: How could you feel more confident going to meet your boss this time?*

Client: *I could make sure I've done my research and reimagine the confidence I felt that day.*

COACHING QUESTIONS

Questions to Challenge Disabling Beliefs

- What makes you feel that way?
- What makes you think that way?
- How true is that?
- What would happen if this time, it was different?
- If it could happen again but in a slightly different, more pleasant way, what could that difference be?
- What can you name the voice that says that?
- If you could, how would you correct what [insert monster's name] is saying?
- What evidence is there in the world to contradict what [insert monster's name] is saying?
- How would you respond to [insert monster's name] if you were being most compassionate and most kind to yourself?
- If you were the kindest person in the entire world, how would you respond to that thought?
- What is another way to look at that?
- How true is that belief?
- How well has that belief been working for you?
- How useful is that?
- How does that belief serve you?
- How have you overcome similar thoughts in the past?
- What are some other ways of looking at this situation?
- What is another way to look at that?
- If [insert challenge] wasn't a factor, what would you do?

- If someone you love was in your shoes and asked for advice, what would be the first thing you would tell them?
- What risk would you take if you couldn't fail?
- If someone you loved said that same thing, how would you respond?
- Who are you trying to please?
- How true is that on a scale of 1 to 100 (100 meaning 100% true)?
- When I shared my observation with you, what came to mind?
- When you figure that out, what will be different for you?
- If you had a magic wand, what would you do right now?
- How could you change that belief to something more empowering?
- What else could that mean?
- How can you rephrase that in a way that honors yourself, your goal, or your values?
- If you could make it more fun, what would you do?
- What could you do to make it more fun?
- What could change about this conversation, right now, that would make you feel better?

Questions to Get Unstuck

- You described what you don't want. How does that help you define what you do want?
- For each of the things you don't want, what is its opposite?
- How can you transform this "don't want" into a positive goal?
- What is the opposite of what you don't want?
- How does this help you better identify what you *do want*?
- Now that you eliminated these choices, what other options might there be?
- What characteristics don't you like? Now, what are the opposite of those characteristics?

ICF CORE COMPETENCIES

Reverse gear is one of the most transformational gears. To be successful, practice:
- Coaching Presence
- Powerful Questioning
- Direct Communication
- Creating Awareness

Coaching Presence

When we address your disabling beliefs, I'm demonstrating confidence in working with strong emotions and managing both myself as coach and client. By picking the right tool to address "disabling beliefs," I recognize many ways to work with the client and choose in the moment what might be most effective.

Powerful Questioning

As we start taking a closer look at your disabling beliefs, I ask questions that challenge your beliefs. These questions may evoke discovery, insight, commitment, or action. Maybe you have those disabling beliefs because no one has ever questioned them before. Once they are questioned in a safe space free of judgment, you may be able to break free of them.

Direct Communication

By "Listening for Contradictions," I directly communicate what appears to be conflicting. However, a contradiction is framed more in the way of "how do these ideas or goals connect, if at all," rather than assuming that they undoubtedly conflict.

Creating Awareness

When I challenge your disabling beliefs, I'm helping you "to discover for [yourself] the new thoughts, beliefs, perceptions, emotions, moods, etc. that strengthen [your] ability to take action and achieve what is important to [you]." That's what reverse gear is all about — challenging a potentially unhelpful way of thinking so that you can achieve what's important to you.

Exercise (Chapter 15)

In your diary, write today's date and "Chapter 15" on top of the page.

In this exercise, we will challenge disabling beliefs that might stand between you and your destination or next stop. Maybe you've had disabling thoughts within the last few hours, days, or weeks. Use those in the following questions, or if you wonderfully have had none, then you can make them up for the sake of this exercise.

EARN 1 POINT

1. Write down one your disabling beliefs regarding your destination or next stop. Then write down a question that powerfully challenges it. Consider using any of the techniques, tools, or questions from this chapter.

EARN 1 POINT

2. Write down a second disabling belief regarding your destination or next stop. Then write down a question that powerfully challenges it. Consider using any of the techniques, tools, or questions from this chapter.

EARN 1 POINT

3. Write down a third disabling belief regarding your destination or next stop. Then write down a question that powerfully challenges it. Consider using any of the techniques, tools, or questions from this chapter.

MAXIMUM POINTS EARNED FOR THIS CHAPTER

You earn 1 point for completing each of the 3 questions above for a maximum of 3 points.

Count the number of points you completed and write down the total number on your Scoreboard, as described in Exercise Chapter 1.

CHAPTER 16, THE 10 COACHING COMMANDMENTS

With inspiration from the name of one of the most popular lists in human history ("The 10 Commandments"), I decided to call this list the "10 *Coaching* Commandments."

This chapter lists "commandments" for every coach to follow.

While the "20 Principles of Personal Change" in Chapter 4 introduced the *theory or beliefs* needed for personal change, now the following list of 10 Coaching Commandments introduces specific *behaviors, guidelines, and practices* for coaches to support their clients through personal change in an honest way.

A "do not" or "don't" instruction helps us understand what to avoid, and a "do" statement positively directs us regarding what to aim for. So, every commandment has both a "do" and "don't" to help you better recognize a top-quality coach.

COMMANDMENT 1: BELIEVE IN YOUR CLIENTS

DO believe in your clients, not in their goals.

DON'T attach your ego to a client's goal.

Outwardly, my role or professional service is to help you get clarity and take action on your goals, but at an even deeper level, my role is to support you and your potential, regardless of how long it takes you or how many goal revisions take place.

You might say that, as my client, you are *outsourcing belief* in yourself to some degree (outsourcing to me, of course), or perhaps a better metaphor is that you are recruiting *more* belief than you had alone.

So, no matter how many times you attempt to reach a goal and no matter how many iterations needed, I will be there for you to develop more clarity and design smarter, more motivated action until you get what you aim for.

Great success often meets several great failures along the way. You may have heard how it took Thomas Edison 1,000 times before getting a light bulb to work, JK Rowling faced 12 rejections by publishers before her profound success, and Walt Disney was fired from a job because he "lacked imagination."

When a client gets excited or feels strongly motivated to reach their goal, but then their goal doesn't work out within their desired time frame, that news might feel discouraging to me only if my own ego were attached to the goal.

Instead of feeling disappointed, I act as an anchor for my client, believing in my client's ability to use everything as a learning experience and as new information that we use to either bring more clarity or design better action.

I am a coach, and I also have a coach. The one I'm working with (at the time of writing this book) has seen me miss my own estimated deadlines many times.

I kept missing my time estimates because they were estimates for tasks I had never done before (so my estimates were overly underestimated), plus I kept wanting to improve my goal and make it better.

As a perfectionist, I kept moving it ahead several months at a time. As her client and after feeling the devastating weight of my own perfectionism and slowness, I said to her "I don't know how you have any patience with me. I must exhaust you with how many times I keep changing things and how long I'm taking!"

In the most compassionate and sincere way, she replied "I'm here to support *you* and believe in *you*, regardless of when you hit your goals." Her words were such a relief and a profound comfort for me.

Practical belief in my client is the first and most important of all ten commandments, and the next one is second most important.

COMMANDMENT 2: FEEL GOOD

DO feel good and bring the client with you to a "feel-good" place.

DON'T bring or feed negative energy into the conversation.

Feeling "good," in a coaching context, means to feel as though you're moving forward. Depending on your personality type, a sense of "moving forward" might feel positively energizing and motivating or it might feel pleasantly peaceful and calm.

As your coach, with every word I say, I aim to stir up a good feeling that moves you forward toward clarity and action. More simply, my aim is for you to feel good about yourself and your progress.

That means if your energy takes a dive, I pull out all the coaching tools I can to bring it back up.

But coaching isn't psychotherapy. Psychotherapists may stop to investigate the source of trauma and get you to re-feel that trauma again as a part of a therapeutic process. Coaches, however, aim to keep you feeling motivated and as though you are moving forward with life at every point possible throughout the conversation.

If you need to deal with trauma, or if depression keeps you from making progress in conversations, it's important to use the services of a therapist either in addition to or instead of a coach.

As your coach, I also need a good feeling, whether it's calm assuredness or energetic excitement. If I don't have the right emotional state for a coaching conversation, how can I be a cheerleader for your goals? So, to help you feel good as a client, I start the call with a sense of movement.

This is why it's important that every coach has a coach, so that coaches feel the forward-movement of their own lives and are working toward their meaningful and motivating goals.

As your coach, it motivates me to discover what lights you up, and that sense of motivation leads me in the beginning of the conversation. Once I've found your inner fire, I let *that* lead the path of our conversation.

If I let your or my heavy or discouraged feelings lead a conversation, I won't be much help to you, and you probably won't even return to me for another conversation.

Here's an example of this commandment.

Client says, "And then, she said ___. I couldn't believe it! I was so pissed off."

- I *don't* say, "I'd be pissed off too! What would you like to do with this anger?"
- I *do* say, "How much time would you like to give yourself to vent?" or "How can you turn this anger into something that benefits you?"

I aim for every question I ask or statement I make to either create clarity about what you truly desire and feel great about or create action that you feel energized about taking.

Every question, every comment, everything remains intentionally moving forward and feeling great. And yes, that takes a lot of digging and work at times, and that's what I'm paid for.

Here's another example.

Imagine your long-term goal is to find a new career that you love, and you have just finished venting to me how miserable you feel at work and how the company owner is a crook.

After highlighting your strengths by commending you for your patience and perseverance, then I ask any question that is forward-moving, such as:

- How does this help you better define what you want in your next career?
- What can you do to feel better?
- What is your next step to finding your new career?

Here are examples of questions that *won't move you forward*:

- What did he say to you that made you so angry?
- How did he make you feel?
- How can you run away from this mess?

COMMANDMENT 3: ASK SIMPLE QUESTIONS

DO ask only one short question at a time.

DON'T stack questions.

As your coach, I aim to keep questions short and ask only one at a time so you can think about it. Forming long or wordy questions gets in the way of clarity.

Here's an example.

Client says, "I'm overwhelmed by the process of creating this product. I've been working on it for so long, and I don't know when it will end."

I *don't* say, "What can you do to make it less complicated so that you don't get overwhelmed and how soon can you get started?"

I *do* say, "What would you like to do about this?"

Asking more than one question at a time (before you've had a chance to reply) is what's called "stacking questions." Stacking questions is like a heart surgeon and a dentist working on the same patient at the same time; there's no need for it. It's a mess and overcomplicating things.

Break up the stack by separating the two questions. Instead of, "What would you like to do first today, and how will you do it exactly," break it up and ask, "What would you like to do first today?" Wait for a thoughtful answer. Afterwards, if it still makes sense, then ask, "How will you do it exactly?"

Rather than creating clarity, stacking questions creates a sense of rushing or needing to answer one to get to the other. It's hard to get a thoughtful answer for each one.

COMMANDMENT 4: USE CLIENT'S LANGUAGE

DO use the client's language in your question.

DON'T use your own words to paraphrase unless you confirm those words to be true.

When it comes to key moments, I repeat your exact words or phrasing whenever possible. That is because of the fact that, when I say something, the mental images and emotional value I have with those words could be very different than the mental images and emotional value that you attach to those same words.

In short, when you say something and I paraphrase it, I might change its meaning or value for you.

Here's an example.

Client says, "I feel overwhelmed when I have too many tasks at once."

I *don't* say in response, "So, it's hard managing a busy schedule." And that's because the client might say, "No, that's not what I meant. I can manage a busy schedule, but when there are too many tasks without clear priorities, it's overwhelming."

I *do* say, "So, you feel overwhelmed when you have too many tasks at once. What might be a way to reduce the overwhelm?"

Although a word might be very close or synonymous, it might still create a slightly different picture in your mind than you intended.

As another example, a client says, "I want to achieve more goals in my career!"

I *don't* say, "How much money more money would you like to earn?" The client may think or say in response, "I didn't say I want more *money,* necessarily. I said I want more achievement."

I *do* say, "If you want to achieve more goals in your career, what could that look like?"

"Clean Language" is an important and related concept to better understand this commandment. Clean Language was originally developed by psychologist David Grove, who worked with trauma patients. He found that using the client's exact words proved to be healthier for the client, respects the client's own understanding of the world, emotional associations, and reduces misinterpretation.[23]

Clean Language isn't only for trauma patients; psychologists and coaches continue to be inspired by his methodology and use it successfully for clients in general.

COMMANDMENT 5: USE OPEN ENDED QUESTIONS

DO ask open-ended questions.

DON'T ask closed-ended questions.

When helping you get clarity in a coaching conversation, my questions will begin with words such as *How..., How much..., What..., Where..., When..., Who...,* or *Why.* Starting questions like that allows you to think more thoroughly about your response and all possibilities. *Open-ended questions* begin with those words.

On the other hand, *closed-ended questions* often begin with words such as, *Do you..., Which ones...,* or *Will you....* They can also require one or two-word answers, such as *What time* or *What's the name of ....*

Closed-ended questions offer a limited set of options such as "yes or no" or "choice A, B, or C," and when it comes to your goals in life, the problem with that is simply we don't know everything. There may be other answers besides "yes" or "no," such as "yes, if..." or "no, if..." or "it depends on timing."

There may be options beyond choices A, B, or C that you or I don't know about. There may be a version of choice A that we haven't explored or yet know about, and that option might be the solution you need.

That's why open-ended coaching questions are necessary when getting clarity on what you need or want in your life. Open-ended questions remove the illusion or assumption that there is one absolute and limited number of choices.

One hack to easily convert a closed ended question to open is to simply add "or something else" to the list of known options, since this opens up other possibilities. For example, instead of asking, *Would you like A or B,* you can instead ask, *Would you like A or B or something else?*

Another similar hack is to add "if any" to the question, such as "Which of these, if any, do you prefer?"

Here are some more general questions that illustrate how to convert closed to open.

Yes or No
Closed: "May I make an observation?"
Open: "How would you feel if I stopped to make an observation?"

Short Answers
Closed: "What day this week would you like to do that?"
Open: "When would you like to do that?

Multiple Choice
Closed: "Would you like A or B?"
Open: "Would you like A or B, or would you like to brainstorm additional options?"

Single Option
Closed: "Would you like vanilla ice cream?"
Open: "What flavor of ice cream would you like?"

In general, closed-ended questions can limit our ability to find the best answers to life's questions. There is a place and a need for closed-ended questions, but only in technical parts of the conversation when confirming logistics, facts for the sake of clarity, or technicalities of the coaching conversation or the coaching contract.

Here are some examples.

- Scaling questions, because they specifically require answering with a score of 1-10
- Technical issues, such as, "Is your internet working?", "Can you hear me? There is a little static on the line," or "Do you mind if I switch from phone to laptop real quick?"
- Confirming scheduled dates and times of conversations
- Confirming you understand the coaching contract
- Permission questions, such as, "Do I have your permission to...?"

- Confirming that I understand you correctly, such as, "I want to make sure I heard you correctly. Did you say...?"
- Asking you to repeat something if I didn't hear you clearly. "I'm sorry, my hearing isn't that great with this cold. Can you kindly repeat what you just said?"

COMMANDMENT 6: ASK GENUINE QUESTIONS

DO ask questions you don't know the answers to.

DON'T ask leading questions.

I ask questions that will improve my understanding of your situation and move you forward toward clarity or action. I ask questions with innocent and genuine curiosity with no expectation of a specific answer.

"Leading questions" are questions I think I might know the answer to or that I ask so that I can hear my expected answer. The danger is that leading questions stall your progress, and there's a sense of the question feeling phony - or even forceful - to one or both of us.

Here's an example.

Client says, "I need to manage my time better. It's going to be hard. My week is already so busy: work, preparing dinner, going out with friends, and then, I only want to rest because I'm exhausted from my day."

I *don't* say, "In the list of things you just mentioned, which one of those things is easiest to cut out of your schedule?" The problem with this response is that I assume this client wants to cut something out of their day. I am leading the client toward *my solution*, not a solution that the client genuinely owns.

I *do* say, "Imagine you were magically able to manage your time better. What would you do first?" In this response, I stick to the client's exact words, and I leave their options of how to fix the problem completely open. This question allows the client to decide whether the solution is to cut something out completely or shorten the amount of time for each event or perhaps add an energy supplement to their day, or something else.

COMMANDMENT 7: CAREFULLY USE "YOU"

DO use "you" in an empowering way.

DON'T use "you" if client feels overwhelmed.

As author of this book, I admit that at the point of writing this book, I consider this commandment the most challenging.

When I ask questions, using the word "you" works powerfully to help you feel like the author of your own choices. For example, an empowering coaching question is, "What else can *you* choose to do?"

Most of the time, the word "you" works well in a question, such as when I am "authoring" (see Chapter 10), which is when I intentionally frame you, the client, as the one in the control seat of your life and decisions.

However, it takes a learned level of sensitivity to recognize when a client needs to reduce an overbearing degree of self-blame.

When a client clearly seems to be angry or disheartened at *themselves*, that's when it's the best time to minimize the use of the word "you" from the question.

It's not that I stop believing in your power to author or change your decisions in life, but it means that I don't want to add any more of an unreasonable sense of self-blame or emotional burden that you may already be feeling. In those sensitive moments, using the word "you" can sound accusatory or judgmental, which is the opposite of what I need to be as a coach.

Here are some examples.

Client says, "I failed miserably."
- I *don't* say, "Why do you think *you* failed?"
- I *do* say, "What factors may have contributed to the failure?"

Client says, "I can't manage my time well and I feel hopeless about it."
- I *don't* say, "Why are *you* struggling with time management?"
- I *do* say, "What makes time management challenging?"

Client says, "I'm not making any progress, it's overwhelming."
- I *don't* say, "What are *you* doing wrong?"
- I *do* say, "What might be hindering progress?"

Client says, "I'm always tired and stressed."
- I *don't* say, Why are *you* always tired and stressed?"
- I *do* say, "What might be causing the fatigue and stress?"

Client says, "I feel totally stuck in my career."
- I *don't* say, "What are *you* not doing to move forward?"
- I *do* say, "What could be contributing to feeling stuck?"

COMMANDMENT 8: ASK WHAT IT MEANS

DO ask what ambiguous words mean before moving on.

DON'T respond to the client unless you first understand what they've said.

"I want to be happier" is an ambiguous sentence. That's because becoming "happier" is going to look very different from person to person, since we often have very different situations and needs.

If you're having a bad day, and you say you want to feel happier, I won't assume that being "happier" for you will mean more money, more laughter, a better relationship, being more fit, or maybe simply a different mindset. Instead, I ask "What does *happier* mean for *you*?" or "What would that look like?"

First, I ask what you mean so we can more clearly see what you might be aiming for.

For example, a client says, "I need to find happiness."
- I *don't* say, "That's a great goal. What's the first step?"
- I *do* say, "What does it mean for you to find happiness?"

My version of happiness could be to cuddle up with a good book and a cup of tea by myself, whereas your version of happiness could mean being surrounded by people dancing the night away.

This commandment does not only apply to "happiness." It goes for any other feeling or aim that's ambiguous, such as feeling peaceful (peaceful in what way or about what?) or being wealthy (how much money and/or assets is that?) or having better relationships (which relationship and improve which aspect?). The list goes on.

Moving straight to a "next step" without understanding your goal is like trying to score a goal in sports by kicking the ball backwards and blindfolded.

COMMANDMENT 9: INTERRUPT, APOLOGIZE, AND ASK PERMISSION

DO apologize or ask permission when interrupting.

DON'T interrupt without either an apology or permission.

In our conversations, 100% of my focus is on supporting you and your goals. So, to keep you and your goals the focus, that means that sometimes, I interrupt to make sure I'm doing my job. In other words, I may not have understood something you said and need clarity, or I may be conscious of time slipping and move the conversation along.

Either by apologizing or asking permission, it makes it more gentle.

For example, a client says, "I'm very selfish to want to spend my life so far away from them. They won't know my kids. And that's just a shame but I also don't control anyone else's life and ..."

- I *don't* say, "Wait, hold on. I would like you to realize you're not doing anything wrong by choosing a life that satisfies your needs."
- I *do* say, "I'm so sorry to interrupt, but I realize we have 15 minutes left, and I want to make sure we're moving in the direction you want. Would you like to continue this topic or return to your goal for this week?"

COMMANDMENT 10: KEEP OPINIONS AND ADVICE TO YOURSELF

DO ask questions that bring out the clients' knowledge of themselves

DON'T give advice or opinions without permission.

A personal coach does not give advice, opinions, or counsel; rather, a personal coach helps you come up with your own genuine solutions, based on your unique values and resources. I help you come to your own conclusions that align with your personality and motivators, as opposed to trying everyone else's.

There are times when I might offer examples of answers to questions I ask, but I only do that to clarify my question. If I sense that those examples are ways of influencing you with my own opinions or preferences, then I have not done my job ethically.

I have coaching tools and techniques to help you identify what you want and plan your unique way of getting there, but my personal opinions and advice are not a part of the equation when it comes to what you want with your life.

For example, a client says, "I'm finding it difficult to exercise regularly. I'm working full-time and simply don't have time! I really want to get fit and know it will improve not only my physical strength but also my mental strength."

- I *don't* say, "What do you think about waking up earlier in the morning or going for a run at lunchtime?"
- I *do* say, "What changes could you make in your life right now for you to exercise regularly?

Running may be the worst form of exercise for you because of a knee problem that I didn't know about. So, I ask you what works for *you*. I help you think through your ideas and solutions that you have in mind, and if you lack ideas, then instead of advice or counsel, I can suggest a brainstorm where any and all ideas are on the table. Then, with your permission, I may offer some ideas for the sake of the brainstorm.

I'm not here to give you my solutions; I'm here to support you regardless of the solution, to make sure you keep moving forward until you find what uniquely works for you.

Exercise (Chapter 16)

In your diary, write today's date and "Chapter 16" on top of the page. This exercise challenges you to practice coaching for five minutes with another person.

EARN 1 POINT

1. Write down the list of the ten coaching commandments that you see in this chapter. For each one, write down the command itself, and then also write the "do," and the "don't." Here's an example of what to include:

Commandment #1 - Feel Good.

DO feel good and bring the client with you to a "feel-good" place.

DON'T bring or feed negative energy into the conversation.

EARN 1 POINT

2. Find someone who is willing to have *only* a five-minute conversation with you for the purpose of practicing two coaching skills. Tell them it's a coaching practice exercise, it's only five minutes, and you will set a timer.

Explain that you're going to take those five minutes to ask them a few questions that help them think about one of their goals.

To earn this point, write down that person's name here and confirm the appointment time that you both agreed to.

EARN UP TO 5 POINTS

3. Your goal for the conversation is to pick two coaching commandments and focus on practicing only those two commandments for the entire five minute conversation.

At the time of your appointment with the person you named, here are five steps to follow.

- (Step 1) Ensure you have the two commandments selected and sitting in front of you before you start the conversation.
- (Step 2) When you start the conversation, thank the other person, start the five-minute timer, and tell them that you have started the timer.
- (Step 3) Start off with one question asking the other person about something they want to accomplish. In other words, ask them, "what is something you would you like to change or accomplish either within the next day, week, month or year?" Then help them get clarity on that step, and discover what they need to do to make it happen.
- (Step 4) Until the timer ends, glance back at the two commandments throughout the conversation so that you can intentionally practice them with every one of your questions and their replies.
- (Step 5) As soon as you end the conversation, write down a few sentences in your diary describing your honest thoughts and feelings about those two commandments that you just practiced.

Complete all five of the above steps to earn five points.

MAXIMUM POINTS EARNED FOR THIS CHAPTER

You earn 1 point each for completing the first and second question, and you earn up to 5 points for completing the five steps in the third question, for a maximum of 7 points.

Count the number of points you completed and write down the total number on your Scoreboard, as described in Exercise Chapter 1.

CHAPTER 17, CONVERSATION STATS

By now, you've read through the seven gears in a coaching conversation (Chapters 8-15), the five assumptions I make about you as my client (Chapter 3), the 20 Principles that lay the foundation for personal change (Chapter 4), your motivators (Chapter 5), and The 10 Coaching Commandments (Chapter 16).

In Chapters 6 and 7, you also walked through the kinds of questions you answer in a coaching conversation, beginning to end.

In this chapter, I offer another way to understand coaching; this time, it's through numbers.

We'll look at the timing and duration of coaching conversations and percentages of what those conversations contain.

CONVERSATION TIMING AND DURATION

First Conversation: Up to 90 Minutes

For the first conversation with a new client, which I call the "destination conversation," there are things to cover that I don't cover in all the other conversations. So, a minimum of 90 minutes is a comfortable time frame for a first conversation or what I call the destination conversation.

Weekly Scheduled Conversations: Up to 60 Minutes

For our weekly next stop conversations, I recommend up to 60 minutes to comfortably allow time for all seven gears. A 2023 global study showed that coaching sessions last an average of 30 to 60 minutes, and they primarily take place over a phone call.[24]

The more time you schedule for a conversation, the more time we have to create deeper clarity and a greater commitment to action. There will be more "aha" moments, more opportunities to discover and challenge a deeply rooted paradigm, more time for brainstorming, more time to recognize obstacles, and more time to design a doable plan of action.

Occasionally, we might schedule 60 minutes but get to the last gear of our conversation much earlier than we thought. In that case, I'll ensure that we've covered everything you need and then end the call early. Other times, we may find that we are running out of time and I have to kick the conversation into the next gears more quickly.

I confirm the appointment at least 24 hours before the conversation time. Once I'm on a call or face-to-face with you, I frame the entire conversation based on our end time, making sure we get through all the gears we need for the day.

My choice and depth of questions fully depends on the time frame. If we're struggling to find clarity, a conversation could go on for many hours. People generally don't have the desire to sit in a meeting for that long, so I keep it to one or two hours maximum and simply make sure to get through all the gears.

I either have a clock visible for reference throughout the conversation or set a timer. As it comes to 10 or 20 minutes before your scheduled time ends, I remind you how long we both have left. This helps focus the conversation and get the most value out of the last 10 or 20 minutes.

Daily Calls: 15 Minutes

I remember when, as a client, I needed 15-minute daily calls with my coach so that they could help me plan my small step for each day as I moved toward my destination. A conversation only once a week was not enough, and one hour a day was too much. So, we had a 60-minute weekly planning call and established what the goal would be for all 15-minute calls for the week. The purpose of the planning call was to use the seven gears format to figure out what I wanted out of the 15-minute calls every morning.

Fifteen-minute daily calls are effective when you have passion-filled clarity on what you want to achieve daily. These calls mostly involve designing actions and maintaining progress and accountability, two of the ICF's Core Competencies.

In a full-length personal coaching conversation that lasts 30 to 120 minutes, I typically spend a significant amount of time in first, second, third, and fourth gear establishing clarity by asking questions that help you figure out what you want that day. However, in short calls, I don't need to spend much time establishing clarity, because it's already been established in the destination conversation.

Because I have learned and practiced the seven gears, I can drive a short call much more gracefully. With a positive attitude, I keep the call moving by interjecting with questions that begin with, "Knowing we have ___ minutes left and that your purpose of the call is ___. What do you think about_?" and fill in the blank with the question that brings us more speedily into the next gear. I have to be very assertive in a 15-minute call, driving you to your goal as quickly as possible without (metaphorically) running off the road!

In short calls, I don't skip gears, but, rather, rely on having already established most or all the gears for clarity in the weekly planning call.

Average Coaching Relationship: Over 6 Months

An ICF global study showed that a coach works with a client for an average of 6 to 12 months.[25] As a coach, I somehow beat the odds, since my first long-term coaching client had weekly coaching conversations with me for an inspiring five years.

As a client myself, the only thing that ever stopped me from working with a coach on a regular basis was my budget. In my perfect world, I'd like to continually have a coach as long as I live.

CONVERSATION CONTENT

100% Focus

When two people have a casual conversation, they are usually concerned with sharing their own original ideas, personal feelings, opinions, and life experiences. When one person finishes, the other person replies with their own perspective and experience. As a coach, however, it's a one-way street. You depend on me to spend 100% of the conversation focusing on your life and progress, not my own.

I must listen closely to what you're really saying and how you're saying it to come up with powerful questions that provoke an emotional response and bring clarity. I take on the role of facilitator rather than advisor or consultant because a personal coach must act as an intermediary between your motivators and destination and the disabling beliefs or negative thoughts that barge in.

80/20 Rule

The focus is on you. This means that, in each individual coaching conversation, I aim to speak no more than 20% of the time, allowing you, as the client, to speak for at least 80% of the conversation.

This means that, for every five minutes of the conversation, I expect you to be speaking, thinking out loud, or reflecting for a minimum of four of those minutes and allow myself a maximum of one minute.

The only exception to this rule is the beginning of our very first coaching conversation, in which I might have the list of coaching agreement topics to cover, what coaching entails, and answer any of your questions about it. If you ask me to introduce any new communication tools, such as a new app for us to chat on, then it may go a bit longer.

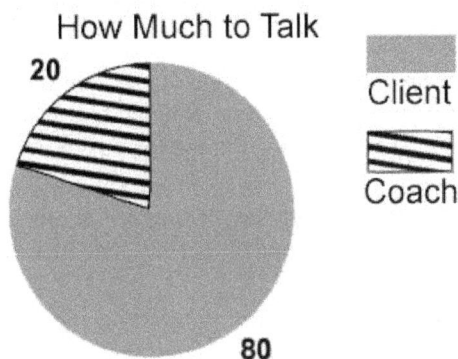

How Much to Talk

- 20 — Coach
- 80 — Client

Coach's Pie

Now that you know that the maximum time I'm speaking as the coach is 20% of the conversation, you may wonder what exactly I'm saying in that time. So, what do I do with my 20%?

Let's imagine my 20% of the conversation as one large pizza pie. What does my "coach's pie" consist of?

Roughly speaking, it's split like this:

- 75% of that pie consist of open-ended questions,
- 20% consist of acknowledgements, validations, observations, or celebrations, and
- 5% consist of closed-ended questions.

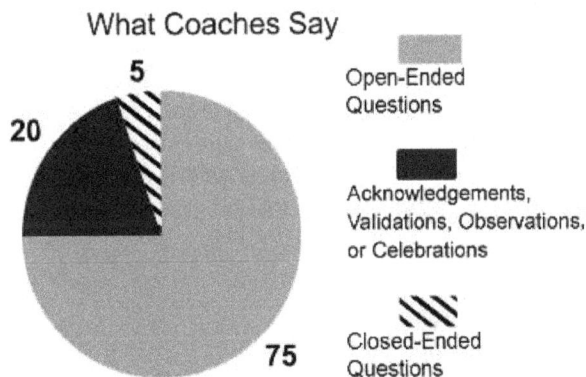

What Coaches Say

- 5 — Closed-Ended Questions
- 20 — Acknowledgements, Validations, Observations, or Celebrations
- 75 — Open-Ended Questions

CHAPTER 17, CONVERSATION STATS
The Science of Personal Coaching

75% Open-Ended Questions

When I do speak, the majority of my time is spent asking open-ended questions. Out of those open-ended questions, I offer two types: powerful questions and meaning questions. Powerful questions encourage you to move forward toward your goal, whereas meaning questions allow you to elaborate on what you mean by whatever it is you've said.

Open ended questions never ask for a clear yes or no, but rather start with words such as "how do you…" or "what do you…," allowing for all possible answers.

20% AVOC Statements

Acknowledgments, validations, observations, and celebration statements, which form the acronym "AVOC," are statements that move you forward. When you read the acronym out loud, it can sound like the word "evoke," a word that means to stir, to call out, to bring back again, or bring something to a person's conscious mind.

AVOC statements evoke your sense of meaning, value, and encouragement. They are typically also followed by an open-ended question. For example, I might use the skill of observation and follow it up with an open question, "I observed a change in your tone. You sound happier now. What do you attribute that to?"

Another example is celebrations, where I might say, "Congratulations on taking that next step. It's something you said you wanted to do for a long time. How, if at all, would you like to celebrate that?"

But AVOC statements also are powerful alone as statements without follow up questions. For example, after you say that you completed something that you were previously scared to do, I respond with the acknowledgment "That took a lot of courage, and you did it regardless of the fear." Then, I leave room for silence after the acknowledgment so you can feel it, process, and respond.

Using AVOC statement also develop trust in yourself and help you recognize your smallest of wins, to ensure no win goes unnoticed; even the smallest of wins carry the power of strong momentum.

5% Closed-Ended Questions

Closed-ended questions, represent only a small percentage of the conversation because they are only used for technical and logistical questions, such as confirming times, dates, internet connectivity, or other quick questions such as making sure I heard you correctly if there was a loud or distracting sounds while you were talking, or if I simply need to quickly make sure I understood something correctly.

When it comes to the emotional content of the conversation, which is usually everything after first gear, I keep away from closed-ended questions because they are restrictive, inhibit creative thinking, and can simply force an insincere answer when it comes to feelings. Closed-ended questions give you less opportunity to think out loud when you need to, and they assume that there are limited options. They have a place in a coaching conversation, but a very limited one.

Exercise (Chapter 17)

In your diary, write today's date and "Chapter 17" on top of the page.

This exercise will help you recognize and become more attuned to some of the types of questions, statements, and conversation numbers we discussed in this chapter.

EARN 1 POINT

1. To earn this point, find a 5-minute video of a conversation between two people or two characters. You might find a conversation clip from one your favorite TV shows, a movie clip, or any YouTube clip. Which video did you choose?

If it's easier, you can find a much longer video and then fast forward to any part with a conversation between two people.

Which video did you choose? Write this down to earn this point.

EARN 1 POINT

2. In the conversation, how many open-ended questions did both characters ask? You can press pause or stop to make sure you count them all, and then write down one total number with "open-ended questions" next to it.

EARN 1 POINT

3. How many closed-ended questions did both characters ask? You can press pause or stop to make sure you count them all, and then write down one total number with "closed-ended questions" next to it.

EARN 1 POINT

4. Give an example of at least one acknowledgment, validation, observation, or celebration statement that either character made during the conversation. Write "none" if there were none.

EARN 1 POINT

5. Think about the conversation and roughly estimate what percentage of the conversation each one spoke. This is only a rough estimate. For example, was it 50% for each? Was one speaking for 75% and the other for about 25%?

MAXIMUM POINTS EARNED FOR THIS CHAPTER

You earn 1 point for completing each of the 5 questions above for a maximum of 5 points.

Count the number of points you completed and write down the total number on your Scoreboard, as described in Exercise Chapter 1.

CHAPTER 18, HOW TO CREATE A SAFE SPACE

Neuroscience research shows that whether the trigger is a bear running after you or a person's verbal attack, when you feel threatened or unsafe, the rational part of the brain starts to shut down, leaving you with only partial brain function for problem solving, decision-making, and memory. Physical and psychological threats create similar impairments in the brain.[26]

So, in a coaching conversation, I want to stay as far away as possible from any question or comment that might make you feel psychologically threatened, and then I can better ensure that your problem-solving, decision-making, and memory are working in their best form.

This chapter shows how I use language to create a safe space for you in a coaching conversation, avoiding words and ideas that may trigger any degree of feeling judged or doubted, restricted, looked down upon, disapproved, or held to a standard you didn't agree to. There are very few places and times in the world in which you can expect this degree of a safe conversation.

When it comes to language that might trigger of feelings of judgment or imposed restrictions, examples might include words such as "should" and "should not," "have to," "need to," "can't," "impossible," and similar.

Neurolinguistics is a branch of science that looks at how words and brain function interact, including how subtle choices in language can affect perception and neurological activity.

The study of an introduction to neurolinguistics was a part of my coach credentialing process with the International Coach Federation, but I do not claim to be an expert. However, I'll touch on related ideas in this chapter. The most significant of which is "reframing."

Put simply, reframing refers to changing language in order to shift perspective. Even what appears to be a minor word change can cause an improved emotional response and a safer or more liberating space to express oneself.

REFRAMING

Here's a quick list of examples showing how I might reframe language during a coaching conversation, all in order to create a safer space that is also open to more or all possibilities.

"Right vs. Wrong" reframed as "Agrees with my conscience, values, or intuition vs Disagrees with my conscience, values, or intuition"

Client: *This plan would be a risk, and I'm afraid I'll come across like I'm stepping on someone's toes at work if I do it. It feels kind of wrong.*

Coach: *What about this plan does align with your conscience, values, or intuition?*

Client: *The part where I tell the truth about what happened is the part I feel good about. Maybe if I just change who I tell, then I will feel better about it.*

"I can't" reframed as "I can if..."

Client: *I can't network. I'm just terrified of random conversations that I'm completely disinterested in.*

Coach: *If we pretend that every conversation you had was interesting, what would the topics be?*

Client: *Well, if I could somehow bring my own interests into every conversation, that would help. I guess maybe I can figure out how to do that.*

"Should, shouldn't, have to, need to," reframed as "Choose to, choose not to, may or may not, prefer, will or won't"

Client: *I hate my job but I have to keep it! I need to earn money for my family. I shouldn't complain, I have a job.*

Coach: *In a perfect world where "have to, need to, and should," no longer exist, what kind of job would you choose?*

Client: *In a perfect world, well, look, I don't know but that makes me think that at least I'd make a couple hours on the weekend to start working on something I love. I'd probably start some form of an online tutoring business.*

"Good vs. bad" reframed as "Helpful, Pleasant, Satisfying vs. Unhelpful, painful, dissatisfying"

Client: *I'm scared of going back into dating and ending up in a bad relationship. I was in a bad situation with my ex-partner. We fought a lot, couldn't communicate properly, and none of our issues ever got fixed, so it got worse and worse, and we finished very unhappily.*

Coach: *What are all of the traits of a satisfying relationship for you?*

Client: *Well, being able to argue respectfully instead of yelling. Having lifestyles more in common than my last partner. And definitely someone who takes the time to talk every day. I need to write those things down to check for them, if I go back to dating.*

"Problem" reframed as "Opportunity, Challenge, Project"

Client: *The problem is I don't like talking to people at the office, so I just super focus on my job and the work I'm doing. But they just keep coming up to me and inviting me to unnecessary chats and events.*

Coach: *What opportunities could arise from this kind of challenge?*

Client: *I'm getting my work done faster than anyone else. I am getting noticed for that, actually.*

"Mistake or failure" reframed as "Learning or building block"

Client: *I failed all my interviews. I made so many mistakes. One time, I was so stressed that I was answering the questions too short and ambiguously, without context. I'm exhausted from all of this, but I need a job in this industry!*

Coach: *What did you learn about yourself from those experiences?*

Client: *I didn't do much investigating into the whole interview process for this kind of role. Next time, I'll be better prepared.*

"Always" reframed as "Every time so far, frequently, or some of the time" (whichever is more true)

Client: *My relationships always fail... I'm very disappointed! I just broke up with my fifth long-term partner. It's always my fault. What can I do to keep a relationship going for more than five years?*

Coach: *I hear that every time, so far, you have been disappointed with your long-term relationships. How true is it that this will "always" be the case?*

Client: *I need to make better decisions so that it's not "always" the case. My next relationship won't be like that if I can make some lifestyle changes.*

"Never" reframed as "Not yet or not to my knowledge"

Client: *I really want to go on this trip but I never want to fly on an airplane. It scares me.*

Coach: *What knowledge would change that for you?*

Client: *I don't know. Maybe if I knew the statistics of plane crashes or if I knew that my flight was with a good reputable airline. Or if I knew that I would have someone comforting me there.*

RIGHT AND WRONG

Apart from legal obligations or an obvious intention to harm self or others, I suspend social ideas of "right and wrong" in our conversation. This means that if you decide to do something that others may judge you for - such as ending a relationship, quitting a job, or changing your mind about something big in your life -I won't judge you as "right or wrong."

Instead, I'm here to support you making decisions that align with your values and motivators.

While it is a rare situation where I would have to even think about this, here is an important thing to note about my legal obligation when it comes to right and wrong. For clients' safety, I do make a distinction between a client's need to vent vs. an intention to do harm. If I suspect a client might endanger their own life or the life of another, then I would refer that client to the appropriate authority.

That said, many people deal with mental health challenges, such as depression, and if you do, it doesn't mean that you won't experience a sense of achievement as a coaching client. As a matter of fact, research shows that combining both depression therapy with coaching can be highly effective.[27]

However, if depression reaches a point in which signs from the list below significantly interferes with the coaching relationship, then it may be better to refer that client to a mental health professional for more targeted support. Here's the Mayo Clinic's helpful summary of signs of depression to look out for.[28]

- Feelings of sadness, tearfulness, emptiness, or hopelessness
- Angry outbursts, irritability or frustration, even over small matters
- Loss of interest or pleasure in most or all normal activities, such as sex, hobbies, or sports
- Sleep disturbances, including insomnia or sleeping too much
- Tiredness and lack of energy, so even small tasks take extra effort
- Changes in appetite — often reduced appetite and weight loss, but increased cravings for food and weight gain in some people
- Anxiety, agitation, or restlessness
- Slowed thinking, speaking or body movements
- Feelings of worthlessness or guilt, fixating on past failures or blaming yourself for things that aren't your responsibility
- Frequent or recurrent thoughts of death, suicidal thoughts, suicide attempts or suicide
- Trouble thinking, concentrating, making decisions and remembering things.

Exercise (Chapter 18)

In your diary, write today's date and "Chapter 18" on top of the page and follow these instructions.

1. Look back to the list of "reframing" examples in this chapter. Let that list inspire you to remember or think of your own inner conversation and which of your own thoughts may benefit from reframing.
2. Think of the thoughts you say to yourself and which ones you could practice reframing. Your inner thoughts that you reframe may come in the form of a complaint or a disappointment or a frustration.
3. In your diary, draw two columns – title the left column "Thought" and the right column "Reframed."
4. In the "Thought" column, list up to five inner thoughts you have which you would like to reframe. For each one, write only one or two sentences.
5. Then, in the "Reframed" column, for each Thought, write one or two sentences that reframe the thought into something encouraging and forward-moving that a professional coach might say.

For each thought that you reframe, you earn one point.

MAXIMUM POINTS EARNED FOR THIS CHAPTER

You earn 1 point for each thought that you reframe, for a total of up to 5 points.

Count the number of points you completed and write down the total number on your Scoreboard, as described in Exercise Chapter 1.

CHAPTER 19, YOUR FIRST CLIENTS

In this chapter, you will take your understanding of coaching to a new level by working on a long-term goal with a client (or several clients) using the theory and practice described in this book.

For the personal coaching experience to be of real benefit, the person you choose as your client will have an authentic desire to make change happen in their life. Otherwise, it will not work.

If you agree to work with someone who is not ready to make a change, that person will not be able to offer the kind of conversation content that allows you to practice your skills, and the coaching relationship will also fizzle out very quickly because it will offer little to no value for one or both of you.

The most powerful conversations are with those who are either motivated to make a change in some area of their life or who are motivated to win in general.

The good news is that deep down inside, many people do yearn for personal change and wish for a safe space to think it through. The challenge is that those people simply haven't yet been offered the conversation space to talk about it or they don't know or trust that such thing exists. That's where you step in.

5 STEPS TO MAKING YOUR FIRST APPOINTMENT

Here are five steps to find the kind of people who are ready to make a change in their lives and who might be patient and willing for you to practice your coaching skills with them. This list of steps is designed for someone who is practicing coaching for the first time or who is very early in their coaching career.

For those who are already seasoned coaches with your own clientele, then you most likely can practice *The Science of Personal Coaching*'s theory, tools, and techniques with your current clients who are already paying for services.

This list of steps below is for those who don't yet have clients or haven't had any or much practice.

Step 1: Make a List

In your diary, find a blank page and, at the top of it, write "Potential Clients." Then, on the blank page, write out a numbered list of friends, family members, co-workers, acquaintances, social media friends and acquaintances, people you know in your local community, business associates, or other human relationships you think of who may want to change something about their lives.

Give yourself a good amount of time to think of everyone and anyone to add to that list.

Step 2: Ask the Big Question

Approach your list of people and ask each one the following question. Here's how.

A. Introduce that you're going through a personal coach training program and are looking to practice your skills.
B. For those who don't know what personal coaching is, you can simply give them a definition as written in this book in Chapter 2.

C. Then, ask each person this important question, *On a scale of 1 through 10, with "10" meaning most important" and "1" meaning "least important", how important is it for you to make a change in your life right now?* If it helps, you can read out loud the twelve areas of life listed in Chapter 9, so that they can more easily think of an area of their own life that they'd like to change.

D. After they give you their score, write their number next to their name on the list that you wrote in Step 1.

E. Only *after* they give you their score, explain that you're looking to practice a couple of coaching conversations with someone who has a score of 8, 9, or 10. You can explain that a person is the right fit for this kind of coaching, only when they have an 8 or above score.

F. For anyone who gives you a score of 8 or above, ask them which of the twelve areas of life they'd like to change, then write that area down next to their score and name on your list.

Then, continue to Step 3.

Step 3: Agree to Conversation Details

A. Cost: If you are new to coaching, then you have a few options. One option is to say that you're doing a limited number of coaching conversations "pro bono," which in a casual sense would mean that you're doing it as a volunteer. Another option is to say that, in return, you'd accept a cup of coffee or similar. And another option is that you can say, "If you find value in this experience, then afterwards in return, you can allow me to use a testimonial," or "... you can tell your friends about my services." Pick any option that you feel comfortable agreeing to, and then be sure to agree to a certain number of conversations or number of coaching hours that this cost applies to. For example, maybe this agreement about cost applies to only three conversations or three coaching hours, then you will review a new cost agreement after those conversations are completed.

B. Time: Ask your client when they can set aside 75 or 90 minutes for an uninterrupted conversation. When scheduling the length of time, it's so much better to schedule more time than you need and end early, rather than to schedule less time and then abruptly have to end the call.

C. Cancellations: As a professional courtesy, ask for a minimum of 24 hours' notice for cancellation or rescheduling as you'd provide the same. If a client cancels or reschedules your first conversation for what seems to be a casual reason, it's highly likely that they are not ready for or able to fulfil the commitment that coaching requires, and I suggest you move on to someone else.

D. Reminders: Send a short email, text message, or make a phone call a few days before the conversation to remind them of the appointment. More often than not, this will significantly increase the chances of the client keeping their appointment with you.

E. Your agenda: Let them know you're new to this and so you will have notes in front of you that may slow you down or cause several "awkward" pauses. Saying that helps both of you prepare for it.

F. Print it out or write it down: On a piece of paper or digital note, write out the checklist items you see in the "Destination Conversation Checklist" in Chapter 23. This checklist contains the topics we covered in previous chapters, and this will be your guide during the first conversation. Do this before your first appointment! For your second conversation with them, use the "Next Stop Conversation Checklist," also in Chapter 23.

Step 4: After Each Coaching Conversation

Within 24 hours of each coaching conversation, many clients appreciate it if you send an email, a text message, or other note with something empowering from the conversation for their reflection, for encouragement, or as a reminder.

A. The best thing for most clients is to simply send a message congratulating them on a specific accomplishment they completed recently, acknowledging one of their strengths demonstrated in the conversation, or reminding them of specific realizations during the coaching conversation.

B. In addition, remind them of what they said they plan to do as their next step. As important as it is to make their goal happen, it's surprisingly common for clients to forget exactly what their next step is.

C. Confirm the next conversation time and date, including a calendar invite if you didn't do so already.

D. Send an exercise that they agreed to complete, if any - one that will help them get clarity about their destination or serve as an extra, optional tool.

E. Some clients ask you to check in with them on a particular goal between scheduled appointments. If this is the case, put the check-in on your calendar with an audible alarm so that you remember to do it.

Step 5: Decide What You Want

After you have completed the couple of coaching conversations that you offered (or however many you agreed to), consider whether you and the other person have enough coaching chemistry, and think about whether they are someone who you'd like to continue working with. Do they genuinely make you excited to coach?

If the coaching chemistry seems good to you, then it's time to let them know that you're grateful for the practice they have allowed you and that you're able to continue if they'd like to pay for your continued services.

If you are new to coaching and you don't feel confident, then it's ok to offer a lower but reasonable price, but only with the qualification that this price is only while you're still learning. No matter what you charge, make sure it's something worth your time.

At the time of this edition of this book, entry-level coaches may charge as low as $50 USD per hour, and high-end coaches may charge anywhere from $250 to $1,000 per hour depending on if they have extensive experience and a strong reputation.

Don't settle for "free." When I lived in New York, I had a friend who graduated from Harvard University and ran a successful non-profit organization. He explained that when he offered courses to low-income communities for free, people did not show up. However, when he advertised a cost in some form, such as presenting it as a scholarship rather than for free, people showed up.

People place value where you place value. They're also more invested in your service emotionally when they've invested in it financially or they believe in the financial value.

Offering services for free has been proven in many contexts to actually reduce motivation in a client and significantly increase their likelihood of making cancellations and being no-shows. Even when training, your time is valuable and worth compensation, and your client will show the value of their time by paying you as well.

Exercise (Chapter 19)

In your diary, write today's date and "Chapter 19" on top of the page.

EARN UP TO 880 POINTS

If you're looking to practice coaching to the point of becoming a professional, it's fairly safe gather at least 100 hours of coaching under your belt, spent with a minimum of 8 different clients. That is one of several requirements I had to meet while earning my credentials from the International Coaching Federation in 2015.

If you have fallen in love with coaching, then I recommend that you investigate the process of earning your credentials through the International Coach Federation (ICF), who would require more items for you to check off.[29]

If you're *curious* about becoming professional but you're not ready to go through the ICF's credentialing process, then this chapter's exercise will prepare your mindset and bring many of your coaching skills up to speed.

The overall goal of this Chapter 19 exercise is to complete both of the following:

1. Complete a *minimum* of 8 (eight) destination conversations, each one with a new client. To earn your points, this must include physically ticking off each box that you see on Chapter 23's "Destination Conversation Checklist" in every conversation. You might tick each box off either on a paper or digital version that you create.
2. Complete a *minimum* of 16 (sixteen) next stop conversations (spread among any number of clients). To earn all points, you must physically tick all boxes that you see on Chapter 23's "Next Stop Conversation Checklist" in every conversation. You might tick each box off either on a paper or digital version that you create.

Each destination conversation checklist has 46 checkboxes to tick in your conversation with a new client, earning you up to 46 points. Do that eight times to earn 368 points.

Each next stop conversation checklist has 32 boxes to tick, so that means each next stop conversation earns you up to 32 points. Do that 16 times to earn 512 points. These next stop conversations can be with any number of your clients.

So that means, if you complete eight destination conversations with new clients and also complete sixteen next stop conversations with your clients, you will earn 880 points for this Chapter 19 Exercise.

As the author of this book, I designed these exercises so that after you earn 880 or more points for this Chapter 19 exercise and have successfully completed all other chapter exercises in this book, then you have developed the conversation skills required to coach at a professional level.

How do you keep track of your points?

On your Scoreboard, where you've been collecting your points for each chapter's exercise, write "Chapter 19" in the first column, but leave the second column blank (where your number of points go). Leave it blank until you earn as many destination and next stop conversation points that you wish to include.

And where do you record your points earned for each of your destination and next stop conversations? The answer is in a client log you create in your diary.

In your diary, set aside a couple of pages to draw the following table and columns - or - create a new and separate digital document (stored somewhere safely) where you can insert a table with columns - or - simply use a pen and paper (once again, stored somewhere safely). Once you have decided on that, do the following.

On the top of a blank page, write the title "Client Log," then underneath, create four columns with the following column titles:

- "Client" which should include the client's name or a unique identifier, respectful of any terms in your confidentiality agreement.
- "Date" which should show the date of each conversation you complete with the client.
- "Type" which should say either "destination" or "next stop," making it clear which of those two checklists you used in the conversation.
- "Points" which should tally how many of the boxes you ticked from the conversation checklist that you used.

If you would like to keep track of your time spent practicing, you can optionally add a fifth column called "Minutes" so you can track your time spent. When it comes to next stop conversations, they typically can last anywhere from 15, 30, 45, 60, to 90 minutes. If you plan to become professional at this or earn professional credentials, then I do strongly suggest adding this column.

MAXIMUM POINTS EARNED

You earn 1 point each for checking off 46 checkboxes in the destination conversation with new clients, and you earn 1 point each for checking off 32 checkboxes in the next stop conversation checklists.

If you meet this exercise's minimum of 8 destination conversations (46 points x 8) with new clients and 16 next stop conversations (32 points x 16), then you will earn 880 points.

After you complete each one of your digital or printed checklist pages, put a date on it and save it. This way you can look back at what you've done and feel proud, and by doing this, you can make sure you've kept an accurate record.

After you have recorded all your points in your Client Log, then count those points and write down the total number in the Chapter 19 row of your Scoreboard.

CHAPTER 20, THE TRIPLE A RATED COACH™

WHAT IS A TRIPLE A RATED COACH™?

I've formulated an easy and wholistic rating system that looks at the aptitude, accessibility, and ability of a coach to establish the coach's individual reputation and integrity.

The Triple A Rated Coach™ rating system, or sometimes called the AAA Rated Coach™, allows potential clients to evaluate a coach's professional reputation and track record, and this system also allows coaches to have a clear measurable goal to aim for when it comes to making their clients happy.

WHAT QUALITIES MAKE A TRIPLE A RATED COACH™?

Each of the three scored qualities begins with an A: aptitude, accessibility, and ability. Each quality gets analyzed and rated by the client in a survey, only after they have had at least two verified coaching conversations.

While many professional services are rated after only one experience, the Triple A Rated Coach requires at least two conversations in order to give time for the coach to demonstrate their accessibility before and between conversations.

Aptitude

Aptitude refers to a coach's natural tendency to empower a client. For example, while a shorter person can succeed in basketball, a tall person might have a much easier and natural tendency to reach the basket and make a slam dunk. Likewise, some people have a more natural tendency to sense the needs of the person they are speaking with.

Accessibility

Accessibility refers to the availability and responsiveness of a coach when a client attempts to contact them or make a booking. This may depend on the number of technologies that the coach is willing and able to manage, and it also depends on the coach's ability to manage their own time and schedule.

Ability

Ability refers to whether a client believes that the coach has brought the client through the coaching process with skilled competency. Clients don't know the technical process or the ICF Core Competencies or the seven gears of coaching conversations, but by answering a few basic questions, clients can easily verify if those basic skills were demonstrated.

HOW DO RATINGS WORK?

What are the rules?

As a coach, after your client completes a **minimum of two coaching conversations** with you, you can ask your client if they are willing to complete a survey rating that helps with your professional development and helps identify your current strengths.

Look at your score as an opportunity to learn about yourself, grow, and gain awareness of those factors or traits that come easy for you. You can name and use those strengths to promote your services, because they are backed by your clients.

Of course, you will also have an opportunity to identify and then master any of the areas in which you may not feel confident. Your lower scores reveal where it makes sense to focus your time, effort, and development.

After their first rating, a client can complete the survey again at any time after each conversation, as long as there is **no more than one rating between conversations**. The more client ratings over time, the more accurate your score will reflect your current strengths.

To keep a coach's reputation and integrity status most current, a client's feedback must be **given within thirty-one (31) days** of the most recent live coaching conversation. If it is found that a client completes a survey more than thirty-one (31) days past your last coaching conversation, then that client's score should be invalidated or deleted.

When learning coaching and doing pro bono or practice conversations, you can choose to personally and privately collect scores so that you can recognize which areas to work on and so you can learn what clients think and feel about your coaching. However, those scores that you directly collect are **unofficial or unauthorized until your client submits their scores directly through Convosique** (the company that published this book) or through an official brand owned by or legally contracted with Convosique.

How are the rating categories weighted?

Aptitude counts for 3 out of 10 points, which is 30% of the total points.

Accessibility counts for 3 out of 10 points, which is 30% of the total points.

Ability counts for 4 out of 10 points, which is 40% of the total points.

"Ability" is given 10% more weight in the final rating. That is because skills and techniques are slightly more important than aptitude and accessibility. Aptitude and accessibility are a little harder to change, while skills and techniques can compensate for the other two areas when done correctly.

How can I improve an "aptitude" if it is something I'm born with?

Two out of three metrics for coaches (ability and accessibility) are areas that a coach can often easily improve, but how can a coach improve a natural inclination or something the coach has had since a child?

You can improve an aptitude by finding techniques and tools that help compensate.

For example, if my voice has "always been monotone" which makes me sound bored or angry with my client (even though I'm inwardly very excited for my client), I can invest extra time and attention practicing how I deliver AVOC statements – acknowledgments, validations, observations, and celebrations.

As another example, if I naturally tend to be risk-adverse and feel a distracting impulse to protect my clients from risks, then I may find it hard to challenge my clients or help them learn from failures. To compensate, I can hire a mentor coach to help me identify the best coaching techniques to overcome that impulse.

Improving aptitude involves identifying the specific areas where you uniquely need support and then identifying and leveraging resources to enhance your strengths in a way that reduces weakness.

It's like having a bad back but going to the gym to build your core muscles. Building those core muscles can alleviate or eliminate the back pain. You find the right movement, put in the work, and suddenly, what was once a weakness becomes a strength. That's how you turn natural tendencies or natural coaching weaknesses into coaching gold.

Do old scores stay in the rating?

Yes. After providing a score, each client's rating remains permanently on record and is averaged into a coach's history. Keeping all old scores in a coach's calculation allows the score to remain honest and tell the true history of the coach's history of client relationships.

As a coach strengthens their weaknesses, the coach benefits from seeing their score rise over time.

THE TRIPLE A RATED COACH™ SURVEY

Here are the Triple A Rated Coach questions given to a client, according to the rules described earlier in this chapter.

For each question below, ask your client to give you a score on a scale of 1 to 10. A score of 10 means "it couldn't be any better" and 1 means "it couldn't be any worse."

Aptitude (Natural Tendency)

1. How much do you feel that your coach sincerely believes in you?
2. How comfortable does your coach seem to feel during the coaching conversation?
3. Overall, how much better do you feel right after conversations with your coach?

Accessibility (Availability and Responsiveness)

4. How easy is it to find an available appointment time on your coach's calendar?
5. How quickly does your coach reply to your messages, emails, and/or phone calls?
6. How well does your coach show up on time to appointments and keep appointments?

Ability (Technical Skills)

7. How skilled is your coach in helping you clarify what you genuinely desire for your life?
8. How well does your coach help you think through each action or next step you want to take?
9. How much does your coach help you overcome negative thinking about yourself and the world?
10. How well does your coach understand and remember what you say?

Exercise (Chapter 20)

In your diary, write today's date and "Chapter 20" on top of the page, and under that, write the title "Triple A Rated Coach."

EARN UP TO 10 POINTS

Choose one client who has completed at least two live coaching conversations with you.

Write or type out the ten questions on a digital or handwritten page, and title it the "Triple A Rated Coach™ Survey." Then, privately share the page with your client and ask if they have five minutes to give you one score for each of the ten questions on the page.

If you choose to share the survey verbally on a call, that's fine but a confidential email may work better and produce more honest answers.

Remind your client that the more honest they are about their scores, the better it will be because you're still training and looking for which areas to improve.

After you have received the client's scores for each of the ten questions, write down all ten scores, then total them on the bottom of the page. Circle your total score and write "My Current Rating."

MAXIMUM POINTS EARNED FOR THIS CHAPTER

You earn 1 point for each of the 10 questions that your client responds to in the survey (regardless of what score they gave you), for a maximum of 10 points.

Count the number of points you earned in this Chapter 20 exercise, and write down the total number on your Scoreboard, as described in Exercise Chapter 1.

CHAPTER 21, COACHING SPEEDBUMPS

In keeping with the metaphor of driving toward a long-term goal, this chapter is about unexpected speedbumps along the way. Speedbumps are simply a metaphor for feeling slowed down in the client and coach relationship.

Sometimes the speedbumps have to do with how you feel about yourself, the situation, or your client. Sometimes the speedbumps have to do with your client not following the "expected" route to achieving their goals.

Regardless of the reason, reading through the following two lists will better equip you to identify and get past any speedbumps that get in the way.

SPEEDBUMPS WITH YOUR CLIENT

1. "The client seems uncomfortable."

Sometimes, a client won't feel comfortable enough to answer your questions honestly. Some might fake a feeling for the sake of social etiquette while others may plainly express that they don't feel good about the conversation.

If the situation persists, then your client will naturally stop working with you. The other option is that you can refer your client to someone with whom they automatically feel more comfortable.

If you are following the principles you've learned in this book, then the trust or discomfort felt by your client may have nothing to do with your coaching ability. It may simply be coaching chemistry or lack thereof or some strange psychological association that has nothing to do with you personally.

For example, your client may associate your voice, name, or personality with something or someone negative from their past. One coach who I hired to coach me had impressed me with her resume of coaching experience, but once I got on the video chat with her, her mannerisms and voice reminded me of one of my mean third-grade teachers. They even had the same haircut! She had great coaching skills, but I couldn't last more than three sessions with her because of that distraction.

For myself, the comfort must be there immediately when I speak with a coach. It's like falling in love. It's immediate chemistry, or I move on. It may be different with others, but if a client is paying for your time and they still don't feel comfortable, the strong likelihood is that they will move on to a new coach anyway. So, it's better that you address it while you can and refer them to someone you know who might be a better fit for them.

2. "My client keeps saying, "I don't know" to my questions."

Here are some reasons your client might say "I don't know" a bit too much, and here are suggestions for each one.

1. Your client does indeed know the answer to the question, but they're scared to say it and need you to lighten the mood so they feel comfortable enough to share what they really feel.

Lighten the mood with a playful role playing exercise.

2. Your client says they don't know because there are so many options.

Offer a brainstorming session where all possible options are listed on paper and then sorted by priority.

3. Client does not know because your question was not stated simply enough.

Make the question more simple.

4. You may have introduced a word in your question that the client doesn't relate to or fully understand.

Use your client's words in your questions as much as possible.

If your client is saying they "don't know" too often, and it appears to be due to despondency or depression, then it may be time to refer your client to a therapist.

3. "My client has two or three things going on and doesn't know what to focus on in the conversation."

Ask what the connection is between the things they have listed. A single focus often comes from their answer.

Another option is to list all those areas of concern and ask the client which subject would feel most empowering to work on first or which one more closely relates to their long term goal.

4. "My client wants coaching but doesn't know what they want or what they're passionate about."

Challenge your client by giving them an exercise such as a vision board, journaling, or another passion-finding process.

Oftentimes, a picture speaks louder than words, so doing a vision board or any form of one can be incredibly powerful. If you need a reminder on how to do a vision board, look back at Chapter 13. On the other hand, some people are more comfortable using words, or they're not ready for imagery, a creative writing exercise can prove to be a good tool to use for them.

For example, a client who wants to feel happier - but doesn't know what to do right now to be happier - could be given the exercise to write a one-page purely imaginative story about a happier day in the future, describing everything that happens on the day from waking up to going to sleep.

These kinds of inventive exercises often lead to powerful discoveries about reality and will help you to. Help them uncover their destination.

5. "It seems like something's wrong with my client like depression or an anxiety disorder."

When your client does not seem capable of moving forward with their life, it could be a due to any number of triggers such as a death in the family, a loss of a relationship or job, an illness, or another overwhelming event or condition.

Your client may need time to grieve, process the event, or discover the trigger or treatment for their condition before they can work on their long-term goal more effectively.

When you observe your client exhibiting any of the traits listed below, it's time to communicate this directly with your client, noting that you observe those traits and that professional diagnosis or medical treatment for them falls outside of your scope of services as a professional personal coach.

- A carelessness about serious or detrimental consequences

- Overwhelming feelings of guilt
- Unable to eat or significant loss of appetite
- Unable to sleep for an extended period
- Excessively uptight, anxious, angry, or irritable
- Expresses violent thoughts or intentions toward self or others
- Cannot experience pleasure
- Obsessing over thoughts of death, suffering in the world, or suicide
- Persistent sadness, hopelessness, despair, or helplessness
- Unable to concentrate or focus

As mentioned in Chapter 18, research shows that combining both depression therapy with coaching can be highly effective. So, as long as the client is moving forward, even slightly, then it may be worth continuing the professional coaching relationship only as long as it is mutually beneficial.

6. "My client doesn't seem to want to make any changes."

If your client has paid for your services, then they are probably willing to make a change, but the question is *how much of a change* they are willing to make.

Use a scaling question. Ask them on a scale of 1 to 10 how much they desire to make a change in their life. To make a change in their life, a person needs a score of 8 or above. If they answer with a 7 or below, share with them that your services are design for clients who have at least an 8 level of desire to make a change (in any area of life).

You can respectfully and kindly put the coaching relationship on hold for the time being and share that you'd like to re-enter the professional relationship when your client gains the level of desire for change that is needed for your services.

7. "My client's having a hard time with the life inventory."

One reason a life inventory may be difficult is that your client might not understand how to define one of the areas of life.

For example, they may not know how to give a score for "Having Fun" because they don't know if it means a relaxing type of fun or the going out to a party kind of fun. The quick trick is to simply ask them to answer according to their own preferred definition of the word. That's really all that matters - their personal definition.

Another challenge when completing the life inventory might be that your client finds one score for a specific area of life too difficult because the topic is too broad and there are too many subcategories in their mind.

For example, when it comes to Financial Health, your client may have some really great scores for investments but some terrible scores for cash flow. No problem! Simply help them break down and list all of the parts, get a score for each of those parts, and then, take an average of all of those scores. The average score for all of the parts becomes the score for Financial Health.

8. "My client rated one of their areas of life the lowest in their life inventory. It was their lowest number, but they don't want to work on it. They picked a different life area to work on that has a higher score!"

A low number might not necessarily indicate what needs attention first. For example, the life area of occupation or career may be a score of 3 out of 10, but the life area of human relationships is a 5 out of 10. It's up to the client to decide what they want to work on and in what order.

Sometimes a client works on a "higher" scored area because they know that another area of life will boost all scores, including any lower scores. For example, they might believe that working on human relationships will their boost career score.

It may also be that the client is actually happy with a low satisfaction score for a season because they have other priorities at this time.

For example, if a client has no romantic life and is focusing on finances first, then the client's score for human relationships may be a 1 but finances a 6. The client may find it a happier goal to first work on finances, even though romance was far lower.

9. "My client says they are committed to completing their actions, challenges, and exercises, but week after week, they don't complete them."

I find the two biggest mistakes for clients are (1) creating goals that are either not measurable or (2) creating goals that have too many burdening steps.

Neither of those kinds of goals are consistently achievable. A goal that is not measurable is very difficult to achieve because it leaves no evidence of accomplishment. The goal that is too big seems great at first, but often becomes too overwhelming to continue.

The situation is often that, as a coach, you did not walk your client through all of the baiting process steps as explained in Chapter 13. By walking through all the steps, one by one, a client identifies a measurable goal and designs one achievable next step of action.

The baiting process requires walking through all eight steps verbally with your client, and as a coach, confirming you heard your client correctly.

Regardless of the reason for an incomplete goal, the most important next step for a coach is to help your client to gather insights and observations from that incomplete goal. For example - what did your client learn in the process? what would your client like to do differently next time? how can we use this experience to make this week's action better? All of those insights and observations will better prepare you and your client to design better actions in the future.

10. "My client wants to work on things other than their long-term goal."

It's your job, as their coach, to keep your client accountable to their destination throughout all conversations and return to the Destination Conversation to define a new long-term goal, if it needs revising.

Sometimes, there's a storm in your client's life, and a metaphorical power line falls down blocking the road to their destination. Other times, it's not a disaster but a very positive event, such as meeting the love of their life, getting pregnant, or unexpectedly coming into a lot of money that creates new priorities for them.

In other words, more often than not, something big happens that might temporarily defer the conversation so that it seems like it's not moving directly toward your client's destination.

Sometimes, all that your client needs is 10 minutes to vent about something negative or 10 minutes to share excitement about something positive. Other times, your client needs a whole new destination.

After celebrating, venting, or mourning, clarify what your client really wants or needs from the positive or negative situation, and then, compassionately discover what their next steps may be.

Let's look at an example. Your client's destination may be to change careers, and today's conversation was going to focus on improving their resume, but you discovered at the beginning of the phone call that only yesterday, their partner left them and they can't concentrate. They need a separate short-term plan on how to cope with that.

Or perhaps your client's destination is to change careers but you discover that your client just won a small lotto jackpot and now wants to celebrate instead of working on their resume. They need a separate short-term plan on how to celebrate.

Both of the above scenarios are short-term changes that appear to go in a different direction. If those kinds of detours continue for too many conversations in a row, then it's time to question the destination. However, if it's not frequent, then those kinds of temporary detours are natural.

I had a coaching conversation with a client who owns a business. In my first conversation with her, we defined her destination for her business and created a motivated and simple next step of action for her to take.

However, when we spoke a couple of days later, within the first five minutes of the next stop conversation, she said that she no longer needed that long-term goal. She now had a new one because her business had changed dramatically since we last spoke.

That was fine.

I took out my destination conversation checklist and followed those steps to make sure we established a new and different long-term goal. She cried with joy twice in the conversation and felt deeply satisfied by the end.

We discovered a deeper, more fulfilling destination.

The conversation is about your client's journey and the places they most desire to go that keep them true and honest to themselves and that keep them true to what's really happening in all other areas of life.

SPEEDBUMPS WITH YOURSELF, AS A COACH

1. "How do I handle the generic how-are-you-greeting?"

When you start the call, you might find yourself naturally asking the client, "How are you?" and your client will politely ask you the same in return. While some clients might genuinely care how you're doing, the problem here is that there will be very few clients who want to pay for you to share your small talk.

As a coach on a paid conversation, talking about your day is pulling focus away from the client and possibly also changing the mood or even making it awkward at times. Personal coaching clients also are paying for each minute that passes, and they are not paying you to hear about your life.

As I've gone through life and lived in several cultures in the world, the truth about this customary "How are you?" greeting is that, for the most part, people don't actually want to know how you're doing. Instead, when they say, "How are you?" they only typically mean "Hello!" or "Good to see you."

When a client asks, "How are you?" the best answer to maintain client-centricity is to say something that returns focus back to the client. Here are a few examples.

- Happy to be chatting with you.
- Happy to hear your voice.
- Me? I'm eager to hear how your week has gone.
- Looking forward to this call.
- Happy to hear from you and eager to know how you're doing.
- Good thank you; how are you feeling today?

Short and sweet, then put the focus back on the client.

And what happens after you ask your client how *they* are doing? When you ask your client how they are, the client's customary response will likely be an automated answer, such as, "Good," "I'm okay," or "I'm all right."

I encourage you to open up the words they say. Ask them what happened or didn't happen that day that made them feel that way. Come up with questions that get over the *small talk* quickly and straight to the *big talk* about what's meaningful to them.

2. "I feel awkward at the end of the conversation, after we are finished with designing the next step."

Once you've "baited" (used the baiting process from Chapter 13), you're done. It's a moment to celebrate. You can congratulate your client on working through all your questions, thinking creatively, having courage, or acknowledging anything that stood out as most important to them during the conversation.

The easiest way to avoid feeling awkward is to take charge and say, "I am looking forward to our next chat. Talk to you then!" and hang up.

However, sometimes you'll finish before the scheduled end-time, which may feel awkward the first time it happens. If that happens, simply ask your client if there's anything else they want to talk about or if they'd like to end the conversation now and pick back up in the next one.

If they have something else they want to talk about and you don't have time to walk through all seven gears, simply help them get some clarity.

If the conversation is prepaid and prebooked for a certain amount of time, but you finished early, then either (a) remind them of the terms of your contract, that it's the same rate, no matter if the client decides to end early or (b) if that term is not in your contract, then offer to add the time balance to the end of a future conversation.

Sometimes the awkwardness comes from the fact that the client's energy isn't up at the very end of the call. To fix that, I'll sometimes say, "So what is one small thing you can do after we hang up to feel good and get your energy up?" It works. It gives them a good note to end the call with.

Sometimes, the client will say, "I'll get a coffee," "I'll listen to a song I love," or something else that's easily doable.

3. "What if I am worried about my client's risky goals?"

I watched an episode of the reality TV show, Shark Tank, in which one of the contestants believed in his business so much that he was putting his mortgage payments on his credit card. I saw the desperate look in his eyes and wondered, "What would I say if I was his coach and he told me that he wanted to put his mortgage payments on his credit card?"

As coaches, sometimes, we are tempted to rescue the client from what we think is a risky or scary idea. Maybe a client wants to invest a large sum of money or quit their job or express a big emotion to someone important to them.

If I find that I am feeling the weight of a client's decision and then worrying about it, this is a yellow flag for me that either (a) I'm forgetting the 20 Principles of Coaching, (b) I'm forgetting the Five Assumptions, or (c) I'm forgetting our coaching contract that relies on my client's 100% ownership of their decisions and actions.

As a coach, the solution for this fear or worry is to ask the right questions, replacing fear with a pure intention of curiosity and trust in the client:

- What or who does this decision impact?
- What are the worst- and best-case scenarios?
- What will it cost if you go through with it?
- What will it cost if you don't go through with it?

Those questions wholistically look at the situation and allow the client to consider the impact and possibilities.

Of course, if my worrying persists, I'd ultimately have to end the contract with my client on the grounds of a conflict of interest. A "conflict of interest" is when a person's personal interests could potentially interfere with their professional duties or responsibilities. I wouldn't want my own level of risk tolerance.

I don't personally know the Shark Tank contestant I described above, but who knows? He may have a large inheritance on the horizon, and so putting his mortgage payments on his credit card was only a temporary issue.

However risky that was or wasn't for him, after appearing on the TV show, his business became a major success. He received investment from one of the "sharks," and he went on to do very well, multiplying his business into the millions.

If I cannot believe in my client because of my own personal fears, then it's a valid conflict of interest that requires addressing directly with the client. Our clients deserve our belief 100%. As a matter of fact, it's our job.

4. "My client is motivated to change, but I just don't like my client's personality. It's annoying or boring."

Coaching chemistry is key to progress. If you have a conversation or two and find that there is little or no chemistry, your client will be much better served by a different coach who does feel strong chemistry with them. You and your client deserve a mutually empowering relationship.

Freedom goes both ways in a professional coaching relationship. When following ICF's standards, the agreement you set up at the beginning of the relationship will likely establish the freedom for either party to end the coaching relationship at any time.

Sometimes, as a lone coach without a network of coaches, you will feel pressure to keep whatever business you can get, so you put on an act. It won't last. Your client will pick up on any forced sense of rapport sooner or later.

Remove that temptation and create more freedom for yourself by belonging to a coaching network where you can refer your client to someone who you think could serve them better. The benefit of a network is that the other coaches can also do the same for you.

5. "The conversation seems lifeless and logical; it's lacking something."

It's lifeless because you're in head space, not heart space.

Dig deep into what matters to the client. You'll hear the change in their voice. Be curious. Ask questions that get to the heart of what the client truly wants out of life right now and what energizes them. An easy way to do this is to check in and ask what decisions in life are not in line with their motivators.

If you try every angle and can't seem to get any degree of emotional or energetic response from them, it could be that they are normally just an unemotional person and rely more on logic than emotional responses. For that type of personality, instead of "how do you feel," you can ask questions more along the lines of "what do you think."

6. "My client is going on and on and on and on and on..."

As a client, personal coaching conversations are my safe space to do a braindump, where I can just say everything that I'm thinking or feeling at the moment. When I'm the client, I love spending most of my time in second gear, talking on and on and on. My coach interrupts me... nicely and with apologies.

Interrupting is a tricky skill because it must be done delicately and with the right coaching intentions, but it's one of the skills that give the client what they are paying for. So, politely interrupt in situations such as these:

- Client's time will run out if you don't jump in. "To make the best use of your time, I want to jump in and ask..."
- The topic has changed drastically from their current goal. "I'm interrupting just to make sure we're headed in the direction you want to head for this conversation."
- You need clarification on something they said, because you didn't hear it or it was confusing. "Sorry, I just need to make sure I heard you correctly when you said something about..."
- You've been writing down a list of topics that they're covering, and you want to make sure you heard them correctly. "I want to jump in to confirm the list of things I'm hearing you say."
- You note something important, from a coaching perspective, that you want to highlight for the client's sake. "It's important to jump in here and bring your attention to something that's been important to you."
- There's a strong negative spiral and you want to use one of the coaching tools to address a disabling belief. "May I interrupt and challenge you here?"

Your client relies on you, as their coach, to help them client find one passionate focus and make progress on it.

7. "This isn't fun."

Coaching is supposed to be an adventure for you and your client. So, if the conversation feels too difficult, it's a sign for you to consider the following.

- Are you following the 10 Coaching Commandments (Chapter 16)? Rules are what make a game exciting. Check and see which of the Commandments you can practice more and give it another try.
- Maybe it's not fun because the client seems bored. Re-check the client's Readiness Score for making change happen in their life right now. "Readiness Score" is a term I use to refer to their answer to the scaling question, "On a scale of 0 - 10, how ready are you to make a change right now?" (or similar wording). Ensure that their level of willingness and eagerness to make a change happen in their life is a score of 8 or above (out of 10).
- Re-check the client's destination. It may be the case that their overall long term goal has shifted and needs redefinition or reinvention.
- The client might not feel a sense of trust with you for reasons beyond your control, the client might be picking up on your disinterest, or they may need professional services beyond the duties of a personal coach. So, refer your client to another coach, therapist (if necessary), or simply mention that you don't feel that you're the best suited to help with their areas of coaching at this time.
- You may have a speciality area of coaching that you prefer, and you haven't discovered it just yet. If the client's progress or topics are not interesting for you, maybe it's time to discover a better niche for your coaching practice.
- Hire a mentor coach to guide you in making your coaching practice more fun.
- Hire a personal coach to work on the areas of your life that may need your attention.
- If you feel that you have tried everything, but bored or even burnt-out feelings continue to happen with several of your clients, maybe for this current season, it's good to take time off of coaching.

8. "I want to give information to help my client, but, as a coach, I'm not supposed to advise like a consultant."

It's a rule in professional personal coaching that coaches do not give advice, information, or recommendations. But there's a healthy way to do it, and here's how.

It's ok when a coach's opinion or ideas are offered as a part of a brainstorming session.

For example, your client may feel burdened with a legal issue and so you might ask your client, "Who would you like to go to for help?" If you are itching with the answer and it seems glaringly obvious to you that the client's go-to person is their lawyer, for example, then ask your client if they would like your contributions to the brainstorm. Then, if they said that they would like your contributions to the brainstorm, then add "lawyer" to the brainstorm.

It may turn out that "lawyer" was actually not the right or best person for your client, and there was a much better answer to the problem. However, the fact that your idea was only part of a brainstorm removes the weight and responsibility that comes with "giving advice."

9. "I don't feel the flow in the conversation."

Is it because you're new to coaching? If so, then bring the feeling to light by asking your client to be patient with you as your practice a new coaching methodology. Directly say it to your client, and it can often remove a lot of the clumsy feelings that come with learning the process.

Saying "Please be patient with me over these next several weeks as I get more comfortable," can create a light-hearted patience or understanding that smooths out the awkward bumps when learning how to coach.

However, if you're an experienced coach, that's another question. If you've gained experience with at least 100 hours of live coaching and you still don't feel the flow in coaching conversations, then perhaps it's time to focus less on technical process and more on intuition.

I've found that intuition is right 95% of the time, and for the remaining 5% of the time, I'm simply not tuned into it. Intuition creates the flow in a conversation. So, first, tap into your intuition. What does it say to you?

Maybe it's simply a matter of checking your client's tachometer a few times throughout the conversation.

If you feel like something's not right and you can't identify it, then stop the conversation and shift into neutral gear. In neutral, ask the client how they feel right now or ask them if they are getting what they need from the conversation. Their answer might redirect the conversation and give you a sense of flow again.

10. "I don't feel like I'm getting to the core of my client's needs. We seem to be skimming the surface."

The answer to deeper conversation is in asking powerful questions. When a client answers any of your questions, it's important to allow for silent pauses to see if there is more coming and to also ask, "What else?"

Often, a logical answer is shared by a client while the more heartfelt answer is buried. You'll need to listen to the client's vocal patterns (tone, speed, breathing, pitch, etc.) and probe with more powerful questions in order to get it out of your client. For example, "What did that change in tone mean for you" or "I heard you pause when you answered. What happened in that pause?"

Other times, a client is hesitant about sharing the deeper story and simply needs a warmer invitation to share more, such as a simple question, "What else?"

11. "I nailed these skills. Now, I want to do personal coaching professionally! How do I market myself?"

If you are new to coaching, then ask for testimonials from the clients you practiced with and see if they are willing to share your name, your service, and contact info with their friends. That's the simple answer.

Next best is to collect testimonials and gain your clients' permission to share those testimonials via all of your marketing platforms such as your new coaching website, social media, email, text messages, and groups in WhatsApp or Telegram.

The more complex answer is that marketing involves several training courses of their own in subjects such as social media marketing, the art of persuasion, communication strategies, target market research, and even graphic arts. This book focuses on the unique skills required for coaching, not the general marketing skills that all entrepreneurs need.

From my own perspective and professional background in communications, testimonials are first priority, and second priority is finding the right technologies for you. Search for the latest marketing technologies and innovations, as they change at an incredibly fast pace these days.

Because it's hard for most coaches to market themselves successfully on their own, I do believe the future of coaching is to join a coaching network that offers its own unique set of features and benefits to both coaches and clients, something that a solo business is simply unable to offer.

At the time of publishing this third edition of *The Science of Personal Coaching*, I am organizing a coaching network or agency through my brand, Best Kinda Friend (@bestkindafriend). So, feel free to find us and get in touch to see if we offer what you need.

Exercise (Chapter 21)

In your diary, write today's date and "Chapter 21" on top of the page.

This is your final exercise of this book, so here's an all-caps CONGRATULATIONS to you.

EARN UP TO 15 POINTS

Write down three coaching challenges that you personally experience when it comes to coaching conversations or the coach-client relationship.

Then, for each one of those three challenges, write at least one or two sentences that describe a way to overcome the challenge using any of the following:

- The Five Assumptions (Chapter 3)
- The 20 Principles of Personal Coaching (Chapter 4)
- The 10 Coaching Commandments (Chapter 16)
- The Seven Gears (Chapter 8)
- Conversation Stats (Chapter 17)
- How to Create a Safe Space (Chapter 18)
- The Triple A Rated Coach (Chapter 20)
- Or any of the tools and techniques described from Chapters 9 through 15.

For example, if one of my coaching challenges is "I don't know what my client thinks of my coaching," then one way I can overcome it is found in "The Triple A Rated Coach (Chapter 20)." As that chapter explains, I can confidentially send the client the 10 questions and ask for their score so I can learn both my strengths and areas for improvement.

MAXIMUM POINTS EARNED FOR THIS CHAPTER

You earn 5 points for each challenge, but only if you also include a way to overcome the challenge. Since this exercise asks you for three challenges, you earn up to 15 points for completing all three. Count the number of points you completed and write down the total number on your Scoreboard, as described in Exercise Chapter 1.

CHAPTER 22, COACHING WORLDWIDE

WHAT ARE THE CHARACTERISTICS OF COACHING FROM A GLOBAL PERSPECTIVE?

The International Coach Federation (ICF) sets the gold standard in the world of coaching, but there are a few other international coaching organizations in the world, too. So, when it comes coaches who belong to these different organizations, do they all use different techniques, skills, and methodology?

According to one study, it appears that most of coaching organizations teach and adhere to many of the same characteristics, with only some differences.

A research project was conducted by Oxford Brookes University in the UK and involved coaching experts from multiple organizations in the UK, USA, and Canada. Gathering data from coaches around the world, the researchers identified a list of over 80 characteristics that they found in coaching conversations.[30]

Many coaches involved in Oxford Brooke's research were credentialed by the ICF; so, it made sense when I found that many characteristics listed in their research agree with ICF's basic coaching principles, standards, and best practices.

However, coaches who are *not* associated with the ICF also participated in this research. So, while the study produced a majority of best practice behaviors, skills, and techniques that agree with ICF, I also found that a small percentage of items on that list conflict with ICF's international standards or were generally not good practice.

Out of 80 characteristics listed in the study, I found 13 of them that conflicted with what I understand to be the highest standards of coaching. When I share the full list of 80 with you below, I made sure to mark those "conflicts" with an "(X)." Then in the section of this chapter titled "Conflicts," I list the coaching standards that they appear to conflict with.

80 CHARACTERISTICS

1. Coach and client explore the effect of client's choice of words
2. Coach and client explore the client's values
3. Coach and client explore the client's environmental influences (e.g., organizational, family, politics, history, etc.)
4. Coach and client explore the client's underlying mindset (e.g., assumptions, beliefs, stories, etc.)
5. Coach and client explore the deeper meaning of a presenting issue
6. Coach works with the client's apparent defensiveness
7. Coach points out recurrent themes in client's behavior
8. Coach points out potential unconscious motives of the client (out of the client's awareness)
9. Coach and client explore the client's in-session non-verbal behavior
10. (X) Coach invites client to consider other people's perspectives on an issue

11. Coach initiates exploration of client's resources and how they may be leveraged (including strengths, accomplishments, and/or external resources)

12. Coach explores client's emotions

13. Coach encourages client to feel more deeply in sessions

14. Coach encourages client to become more aware of their immediate experience in the session

15. Coach challenges client's perspective of situation and/or self

16. Coach asks client to quantify the feeling/perception/issue at hand using a scale

17. Coach allows for one or more periods of silent reflection

18. Coach and client discuss the results of a psychometric instrument

19. (X) Coach and client discuss external feedback

20. (X) Coach gives feedback from coach's experience of client

21. (X) Coach discloses own feelings/bodily sensations evoked in the session

22. Coach uses metaphors productively

23. Coach and client explore their differences in perception of the situation

24. Coach expands on client's statements

25. Coach provides reassurance to client

26. Coach uses humor

27. Coach shows empathy

28. (X) Coach shares personal details about themself

29. (X) Coach discloses own fallibility

30. Coach and client have a good rapport (strong connection)

31. Coach and client appear to understand each other

32. Coach and client discuss their relationship

33. Coach asks for permission to give feedback

34. Coach repeats client's words back to them

35. (X) Coach paraphrases the client's statements

36. Coach checks if their understanding is correct

37. Coach and client share a sense of optimism

38. Coach and client experience a shift in energy during the coaching session

39. Coach and client appear to be engaged (vs. disengaged)

40. Coach follows up on key/significant statements made by client

41. Coach asks questions to help the client elaborate

42. Coach and client discuss the coaching "contract"

43. Coach and client discuss issues related to the termination of coaching

44. Coach and client discuss boundaries and/or ethical issues related to the coaching engagement

45. Coach and client discuss potential referral to an outside specialist (e.g., therapist, doctor, financial advisor)

46. (X) Coach maintains a fast-paced session

47. Coach maintains the structure of the session

48. Coach and client appear to bring the session to closure easily

49. Coach and client discuss the process of the session

50. Coach takes an active role during the session

51. (X) Coach makes explicit when there is a shift in role during the session (e.g., acting as consultant, teacher, therapist)

52. Coach explains the reason behind using a specific intervention

53. Coach appears to be using an intervention mechanistically

54. Coach appears to be pursuing their clients agenda

55. Coach allows client to take initiative in structuring the session

56. Coach and client discuss client's feedback on coaching

57. Coach makes sounds or non-verbally encourages client to continue

58. (X) Coach is verbose

59. (X) Coach interrupts client

60. Coach encourages client to interrupt them

61. Coach suggests in-session exercises/activities

62. Coach broadens the focus of discussions

63. Coach asks questions that appear to open new possibilities for the client

64. (X) Coach appears to focus on a third-party's agenda [e.g., third parties can be an organization who hire coaches for their staff's development]

65. Coach encourages client to suggest their next course of action

66. Coach and client discuss new practices for the client

67. Coach offers possible solutions

68. Coach suggests homework for client

69. Coach shares their knowledge about topics

70. (X) Coach gives advice

71. Coach follows up on previous homework

72. Coach encourages client to make choices

73. Coach asks the client to describe key learnings/take-aways from session

74. Coach and client discuss the client's progress

75. Coach and client discuss the client's overall goals

76. Coach and client discuss how to measure the success of the coaching engagement

77. Coach redirects client to client's agenda

78. Coach explores client's level of engagement in coaching

79. Coach inquires about client's aim for the session

80. (X) Coach and client discuss the client's impact on their environment (e.g., organization, family)

Well done; you made it to the end of the list.

CORE COMPETENCIES

For over 20 years, the International Coaching Federation (ICF), have maintained their own list of what professional coaching consists of, and it's much easier to digest than the 80 items above. They established an essential list of 11 standards, skills, and techniques (called "Core Competencies") for professionally qualified coaches to uphold.[31]

A professional coach must demonstrate their proficiency in each of these areas:

1. Meeting Ethical Guidelines and Professional Standards
2. Establishing the Coaching Agreement
3. Establishing Trust and Intimacy with the Client
4. Coaching Presence
5. Active Listening
6. Powerful Questioning
7. Direct Communication
8. Creating Awareness
9. Designing Actions
10. Planning and Goal Setting
11. Managing Progress and Accountability

CONFLICTS

Regarding the research project from Oxford Brookes University, which of the 80 items in their list conflict with best practice and recognized standards?

As mentioned earlier, I identified 13 items from the university study which go against ICF standards or are generally not good practice. Here they are.

#10 presents potential conflict with ICF's Core Competencies 1 and 3.

#19, 20, 21, 28, 29, 46 and 58 present potential conflicts with ICF's Core Competencies 1,3 and 4.

#35 conflicts with ICF's Core Competencies 1,3,5 and 7.

#59 conflicts with ICF's Core Competencies 1,3,4 and 5.

#64 and 80 present potential conflicts with ICF's Core Competencies 1,3 and 7.

#51 and 70 conflicts with ICF's Core Competencies 1, 2, 3 and 4.

ANY THERE ANY MORE LISTS THAT CHARACTERIZE COACHING?

By this point, we have established that there is a list of 80 characteristics of a coaching conversation, and we also have the ICF's list of 11 Core Competencies. However, there's a problem.

In this early stage in the history of coaching, neither of the lists and nowhere to my knowledge can we find a repeatable structure and process to follow for every coaching conversation. In other words, when exactly does a coach say something and in what order do they say it?

Neither the above lists - the 80 or the 11 - provide chronological steps or a repeatable process on how to start and end a coaching conversation. Neither one directs a coach on the route to follow when feeling lost in the conversation. So, how can coaches feel and know that they are on track?

Because of that gap in training, many coaches find themselves feeling lost somewhere in the middle and end of a coaching conversation.

Early on, I experienced that sense of loss and confusion, and it's frustrating when you're meant to be the professional. So, because I love coaching and feel compelled to make the experience repeatable by all who learn it, I formulized the process in this book and used the metaphor of "the seven gears," as you have learned by now.

My hope is that those seven gears will be the final - or even the only - list that anyone will need for powerful coaching conversations.

CHAPTER 23, CHECKLISTS

Good news! You don't need to flip back and forth through every chapter in order to find the checklists for a conversation. Instead, I've put them all into one place for you here in this chapter so that you can copy it over somewhere for a quick reference and placed in front of you for every coaching conversation with your clients.

In this chapter, you'll see the two coaching conversation checklists, one for a destination conversation and the other for a next stop conversation.

In every conversation, start in first gear, shift up gears to move your client forward, shift to neutral and reverse when necessary, and then end each conversation in fifth.

However, within each individual gear, you can tick the boxes in any order. For example, in first gear, you might choose to discuss permissions before discussing confidentiality. As another example, in second gear, you can ask about a client's homework before exploring multiple topics before entering third gear. So, don't worry about the exact order of the items you see listed within an individual gear.

Like learning to drive stick shift for the first time, using these checklists will most likely feel clumsy and awkward for you at first. It will most likely be a relief to you and the client if you clearly set that expectation ahead of time by saying something like, "This is new to me, so please be patient as I flip through my notes or take a little long to make sure I'm doing this right."

Direct communication and setting expectations in a light-hearted way with your client takes away most of - and sometimes *all of* - the awkwardness.

It may seem impossible to you right now, but after some practice, ticking off all checkboxes will become natural to you, and you will eventually be able to move through the seven gears from memory.

DESTINATION CONVERSATION CHECKLIST

First Gear
- Confirm today's time frame and any other logistics for the conversation
- Affirm a safe space
- Allow silent pauses for processing

When speaking with a client for the first time:
- Describe client-centricity
- Cover cancellations, lateness, and rescheduling
- Provide coaching definition (clarity and action)
- Cover confidentiality
- Discuss permission
- Permission to take notes
- Effectiveness depends on regularly scheduled conversations
- Review communication technology options for our conversations
- Five Assumptions (knowledge, honesty, resources, false assumptions, emotional ends)
- Your decisions are 100% up to you, not me
- Coach's availability and responsiveness
- Answer any of client's questions about coaching

Second Gear

- [x] Explore multiple topics (braindump)
- [x] Provide acknowledgments, validations, observations, and celebrations
- [x] Allow silent pauses for processing
- [x] Calibrate (discover client's tone of joy)
- [x] Discover your motivators (if not done prior to conversation)
- [x] Discover what you are tolerating in life right now
- [x] Perform life inventory (if not done prior to conversation)
- [x] Review how you feel or what you think about your life inventory

Third Gear

- [x] Find one most passionate change to make in any area of life (aka a "destination")
- [x] Confirm what the change feels, looks, and sounds like
- [x] Confirm how well it aligns with your motivators
- [x] Confirm how that change would be different than your current experience
- [x] Allow silent pauses for processing
- [x] Identify what it will cost if you don't make this change

Fourth Gear

- [x] Type or write client's exact words or phrase for their long-term goal (aka "destination")
- [x] Repeat word or phrase back to them
- [x] Allow silent pauses for processing

Fifth Gear

- [x] The Bang
- [x] The Baby Step
- [x] The Backlog
- [x] The Booking
- [x] The Banking
- [x] The Battle
- [x] The Belief
- [x] The Backbone
- [x] Allow silent pauses for processing

Neutral Gear

- [x] Check if you are ready to shift up a gear (tachometer)
- [x] Check which gear we need to shift down to, if needed (tachometer)
- [x] Allow silent pauses for processing

Reverse Gear

- [x] Identify and challenge disabling beliefs.
- [x] Convert "I don't want" to "what I do want."
- [x] Allow silent pauses for processing

<u>NEXT STOP CONVERSATION CHECKLIST</u>

First Gear
- [x] Confirm today's time frame and any other logistics for the conversation
- [x] Affirm a safe space
- [x] Allow silent pauses for processing

Second Gear
- [x] Explore multiple topics (braindump)
- [x] Ask about completed homework and/or what they learned in the process
- [x] Provide acknowledgments, validations, observations, and celebrations
- [x] Allow silent pauses for processing

Third Gear
- [x] Find one most passionate change or action to complete between now and our next conversation (aka a "next stop")
- [x] Confirm what the change feels, looks, and sounds like
- [x] Confirm how well it aligns with your motivators
- [x] Confirm what would be different than your current experience
- [x] Identify how this change progresses the journey to your destination
- [x] Allow silent pauses for processing
- [x] Identify what it will cost if you don't take this next step

Fourth Gear
- [x] Type or write client's exact words or phrase for their short-term goal (aka "next stop")
- [x] Repeat word or phrase back to them
- [x] Allow silent pauses for processing

Fifth Gear
- [x] The Bang
- [x] The Baby Step
- [x] The Backlog
- [x] The Booking
- [x] The Banking
- [x] The Battle
- [x] The Belief
- [x] The Backbone
- [x] Allow silent pauses for processing

Neutral Gear
- [x] Check if you are ready to shift up a gear (tachometer)
- [x] Check which gear we need to shift down to, if needed (tachometer)
- [x] Allow silent pauses for processing

Reverse Gear
- [x] Identify and challenge disabling beliefs.
- [x] Convert "I don't want" to "what I do want."
- [x] Allow silent pauses for processing

ENDNOTES

1. Couto, Diane, & Kauffman, Carol. (2009, January). What can coaches do for you? Harvard Business Review.
Retrieved from: http://hbr.org/2009/01/what-can-coaches-do-for-you

2. International Coach Federation. About.
Retrieved from: https://coachfederation.org/about

3. David, Susan. (2017, November.) The gift and power of emotional courage. TED. Retrieved from:
https://www.ted.com/talks/susan_david_the_gift_and_power_of_emotional_courage/transcript#t-418277

4. Information gathered from the following sources:
Peterson, Christopher, & Sellgman, Martin. (2004.) Character strengths and virtues: a handbook and classification. Washington, DC: American Psychological Association.

VIA Institute on Character. (2018, April.) Character strengths and achievement. Retrieved from:
http://www.viacharacter.org/www/Research/Research-Findings-Character-Strengths-and-Achievement

VIA Institute on Character. The VIA classification of strengths. Retrieved from:
http://www.viacharacter.org/www/Portals/0/VIA%20Classification%202017.pdf

5. Guay, Russel, & Parks-Leduc, Laura. (2009, June.) Personality, values, and motivation. Personality and Individual Differences, 24, 675-684.
Retrieved from:
https://www.researchgate.net/publication/222513052_Pesonality_values_and_motivation

6. International Coach Federation. ICF global coaching client study: executive summary.
https://coachfederation.org/app/uploads/2020/09/FINAL_ICF_GCS2020_ExecutiveSummary.pdf

7. McCoy, Cyndi. "Shifting through the Seven Gears of a Coaching Conversation." International Coaching Federation, 22 April 2019, https://coachingfederation.org/blog/seven-gears-of-coaching-convo.

8. Willis, Janine, and Alexander Todorov. "First Impressions: Making up Your Mind after a 100-ms Exposure to a Face." Psychological Science 17, no. 7 (2006): 592–598. https://doi.org/10.1111/j.1467-9280.2006.01750.x.

9. Wargo, Eric. (2006, July.) How many seconds to a first impression? Observer Magazine. Retrieved from:
https://www.psychologicalscience.org/observer/how-many-seconds-to-a-first-impression&sa=D&ust=1544364931259000&usg=AFQjCNHXdD_Kjkqr7MLpZbqehr5SJ4cCAw

10. Campbell, Kelly. (2011, August.) Relationship chemistry: Can science explain instant connections? Psychology Today. Retrieved from:
https://www.psychologytoday.com/us/blog/more-chemistry/201108/relationship-chemistry-can-science-explain-instant-connections

11. Information on updates to Core Competencies:
In 2019, ICF reorganized the 11 Core Competencies to a list of 8, but ICT still requires all 11 original Core Competencies for credentialed coaches. Any competencies might appear to be

removed from the main list have only been moved into one of the other competencies as subcategories or part of newly named competencies. The updated list attempts to simplify the structure.

Coaches Training Blog. (n.d.). New vs Old: The ICF Core Competencies in Coaching. Retrieved from:

https://coachestrainingblog.com/becomeacoach/new-vs-old-the-icf-core-competencies-in-coaching/

International Coaching Federation. (n.d.). ICF Core Competencies. Retrieved from:

https://coachingfederation.org/credentials-and-standards/core-competencies

12. Amabile, Teresa, & Kramer, Steve. (2011.) The progress principle: Using small wins to ignite joy, engagement, and creativity at work. Harvard Business School. Retrieved from: https://www.hbs.edu/faculty/Pages/item.aspx?num=40692

Related article:

Nobel, Carmen. (2011, September.) How small wins unleash creativity. Harvard Business School. Retrieved from https://hbswk.hbs.edu/item/how-small-wins-unleash-creativity

13. Niles, Frank. (2011, August.) How to use visualization to achieve your goals. The Huffington Post. Retrieved from https://www.huffpost.com/entry/visualization-goals_b_878424

14. Maese, Rick. (2016, July.) For Olympians, seeing (in their minds) is believing (it can happen). The Washington Post. Retrieved from:

https://www.washingtonpost.com/sports/olympics/for-olympians-seeing-in-their-minds-is-believing-it-can-happen/2016/07/28/6966709c-532e-11e6-bbf5-957ad17b4385_story.html

15. Ranganathan, V. K., Siemionow, V., Liu, J. Z., Sahgal, V., & Yue, G. H. (2004). From mental power to muscle power--gaining strength by using the mind. Neuropsychologia, 42(7), 944-956. Retrieved from https://pubmed.ncbi.nlm.nih.gov/14998709/

16. Adams, A. J. (2009, December.) Seeing is believing: The power of visualization. Psychology Today. Retrieved from: https://www.psychologytoday.com/au/blog/flourish/200912/seeing-is-believing-the-power-visualization

17. Szczypka, M. S., Rainey, M. A., Kim, D. S., Alaynick, W. A., Marck, B. T., Matsumoto, A. M., & Palmiter, R. D. (1999). Feeding behavior in dopamine-deficient mice. Proceedings of the National Academy of Sciences of the United States of America, 96(21), 12138-43. Retrieved from: https://www.ncbi.nlm.nih.gov/pmc/articles/PMC18425/

18. Study focuses on strategies for achieving goals, resolutions. (2015, May.) Retrieved from the Dominican University of California News Room website:

https://web.archive.org/web/20190216101420/https://www.dominican.edu/dominicannews/study-highlights-strategies-for-achieving-goals.

19. Oxford University Press. (2018.) OED Online. Retrieved from

https://en.oxforddictionaries.com/definition/motivation.

20. Snyder, C. R. "Hope Theory: Rainbows in the Mind." Psychological Inquiry 13, no. 4 (2002): 249–275. https://doi.org/10.1207/S15327965PLI1304_01.

21. Gersten, Dennis, and Roger Mazlen. "Amino Acids." CFS Radio Program, February 1998. Accessed July 18, 2024.

https://web.archive.org/web/20240705231323/https://www.imagerynet.com/amino/audio/amino.audio.txt.html. More information on Dr. Gersten can be found at Psychology Today: https://www.psychologytoday.com/us/psychiatrists/david-gersten-carlsbad-ca/342493.

22. Wegner, D. M., Schneider, D. J., Carter, S. R., & White, T. L. (1987). Paradoxical effects of thought suppression. Journal of Personality and Social Psychology, 53(1), 5-13. Retrieved from http://psycnet.apa.org/record/1987-33493-001

23. Grove, David. *Clean Language: Revealing Metaphors and Opening Minds*. Crown House Publishing, 2000.

24. International Coaching Federation. *2023 ICF Global Coaching Study*. International Coaching Federation, 2023.
https://researchportal.coachingfederation.org/Document/Pdf/1565.pdf

25. (See ICF Global Coaching Study in endnote number 24.)

26. Eisenberger, Naomi I. "The Neural Bases of Social Pain: Evidence for Shared Representations With Physical Pain." Nature Reviews Neuroscience 13, no. 6 (2012): 421-434. Accessed July 23, 2024.
https://sanlab.psych.ucla.edu/wp-content/uploads/sites/31/2015/05/Eisenberger2012PsychosamaticMed.pdf.

27. Ammentorp, Jette, Lisbeth Uhrenfeldt, Flemming Angel, Martin Ehrensvärd, Ebbe B Carlsen, and Poul-Erik Kofoed. "Can Life Coaching Improve Health Outcomes? – A Systematic Review of Intervention Studies." *BMC Health Services Research* 13, no. 428 (2013). https://doi.org/10.1186/1472-6963-13-428.

28. Depression (major depressive disorder). Retrieved from the Mayo Clinic website: http://www.mayoclinic.org/diseases-conditions/depression/basics/symptoms/con-20032977.

29. International Coaching Federation. "How to Apply for Credentials and Standards." International Coaching Federation, accessed July 24, 2024. https://coachingfederation.org/credentials-and-standards/how-to-apply.

30. Bachkirova, Tatiana, Jonathan Sibley, and Adrian Christopher Myers. "Developing and Applying a New Instrument for Microanalysis of the Coaching Process: The Coaching Process Q-Set." Human Resource Development Quarterly 26, no. 4 (2015): 431-462. Note: In the list of 80 Characteristics in Chapter 22, a minor number words or items were modified for the sake of improved readability or clarity.

31. (See above endnote number 11 regarding the reorganization of the Core Competencies.)

192

ABOUT THE AUTHOR

I don't usually enjoy talking about myself in the third-person, but here we go.

Cyndi was born in New York City and, as an adult, lived in England for a year, Israel for five months, and California for under two years. She lived in different parts of New York for much of her life until 2013, when Cyndi travelled from an apartment where she lived in Staten Island, NYC, to the country of Australia which eventually become her new home.

Back in her high school days, Cyndi won a number of awards for her multi-media artwork, including a Gold Key to New York State, an Eastman Kodak scholarship, and a scholarship from her high school. She was offered acceptance to the School of Visual Arts in Manhattan and later offered a full scholarship to a college in Kentucky, but she rejected both options thinking of Kentucky as too quiet and Manhattan as too frantic.

Cyndi has analyzed life since childhood, passionately asking big questions such as, "Why should I?" when her parents asked her to do things that she didn't want to do. She finally found the right context for life's big questions at university where she studied philosophy, graduating from a private Christian college with highest honors and spending one year at the University of Oxford, Keble College in England for her junior year.

In her career, Cyndi has also worked in professional communications roles at several multibillion-dollar companies, mostly focused on technology and transformation.

As for coach training, she successfully completed the International Coach Federation's credentialing process in 2015. She also completed three different coach training programs, including Life and Leadership Potentials training from the Institute for Professional Excellence in Coaching (iPEC), Certified Coach training from Fowler Wainwright International, and third, Holistic Life, Career & Executive Coach Training from Goal Imagery Institute.

Coaching helps her keep true to her greatest loves.

Finally, Cyndi also wrote a book titled *The Boundaries Health Check* and published an app with the same name to go with it. The Boundaries Health Check book and app help you name, measure, and track the health of your boundaries, and you can find it online by searching @boundariescheck or searching the title itself.

Her coaching brand is "Best Kinda Friend," which you can also find on social media as @bestkindafriend.

ACKNOWLEDGMENTS

Thank you to everyone who helped me make this book happen.

Martha, for your professional coaching, feedback, encouragement, and patience as I thought through many iterations of this book.

Charlotte, for being there in the beginning to help keep it going when my motivation was at its very lowest.

Michael, mentor coach, for that one specific coaching session that was absolutely pivotal for me to get this book finished and for inspiring me to develop the technique - Listening for Contradictions.

Liz aka "Woman," for taking a look and giving feedback.

The Gray family, for your significant encouragement and support early on.

All my friends, family, and Facebook friends for your many words of encouragement that renewed my motivation.

Joshua, for your loving and unwavering support in everything I do.

And, finally, to the miracle man from 2,000 years ago who said, "What do you mean, 'If I can'? Anything is possible if a person believes." (Mark 9:23)